The *Battle of Gettysburg* Cyclorama

A History and Guide

The
Battle of Gettysburg
Cyclorama

A History and Guide

By Sue Boardman and Kathryn Porch

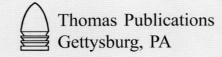

Thomas Publications
Gettysburg, PA

Published by   THOMAS PUBLICATIONS
                P.O. Box 3031
                Gettysburg, Pa. 17325

ISBN-978-1-57747-138-7

Contents

Acknowledgements

The authors would like to thank the following individuals for their assistance and support: Brad Graham; Eric Dennis; Dean Knudsen; Brion Fitzgerald; Don Johnson; Susanne Wray; Gordon Jones; Scott Hartwig; Dean Thomas; Jim Thomas; David Olin; Beth Trescott; Charles Berkey; Perry Huston; Ken Boardman; Brent LaRosa; John Heiser; Barbara Finfrock; Susan Corbett.

Introduction

The *Battle of Gettysburg* Cyclorama captures a seminal moment in the history of the Civil War: the moment on the afternoon of the July 3, 1863, when the Confederate attack reached the Union lines on Cemetery Ridge. The moment depicted has often been referred to as the "High Tide of the Confederacy," a tide that crested on that now-famous ridge, signaling a subtle turning point in the fortunes of the Union army. Although the war continued for an additional two years, the climactic event known as "Pickett's Charge" inspired historians, poets and artists of past generations like no other. The massive *Battle of Gettysburg* cyclorama captures the charge in all of its grand and tragic pageantry.

The perspective of the painting allows the observer to be directly in the center of this charge. The viewer is positioned just behind the Union Line, on the crest of the ridge, just above the action. From this vantage point viewers can see key figures of the battle as well as important landmarks. They have a remarkable position from which to witness this moment in history, frozen in time.

Within these pages you will learn about many aspects of this painting. You will learn about the seminal battle that inspired it, the technical aspects and science behind the cyclorama genre, and the history of cycloramas in general and the Gettysburg Cyclorama in particular. Perhaps most fascinating, you will learn about the history connected to Gettysburg National Military Park's version of the *Battle of Gettysburg* Cyclorama and its journey from Boston to Gettysburg where it can be seen today.

CHAPTER 1

An Historic Charge, Captured on Canvas

Excerpted from: "The Gettysburg National Military Park Virtual Tour: The Story of the Battle of Gettysburg" by John Heiser, Librarian and Historian, Gettysburg National Military Park

The Battle of Gettysburg was a turning point in the American Civil War. The Union victory in the summer of 1863 ended General Robert E. Lee's second and most ambitious invasion of the North. Often referred to as the "High Water Mark of the Confederacy," it was the war's bloodiest battle with 51,000 casualties. It also provided President Abraham Lincoln with the setting for his most famous address.

The Civil War in Its Third Year

Fought during the first three days of July 1863, the Battle of Gettysburg was one of the most critical battles of the war and occurred at a time when the fate of the nation hung in the balance. Despite promising victories on the battlefield in 1862, the Union cause had suffered several reversals most notably in the eastern theater. The Confederacy's most victorious army, the *Army of Northern Virginia*, had successfully thwarted numerous Union threats against the Confederate capitol of Richmond. Outnumbered and out gunned, this army, under the guidance of General Robert E. Lee, had won strategically important victories at Fredericksburg in 1862 and Chancellorsville, Virginia, in May 1863. By that June, Lee's army enjoyed a surge of confidence in itself having frustrated the much larger Union *Army of the Potomac*, and the high casualties that resulted cast a pall over the North. President Lincoln had appointed commander after commander to no avail; Lee defeated each and every one. There was one bright spot for the Union cause that summer – the Union Army under General Ulysses S. Grant had encircled Vicksburg, Mississippi, the last great Confederate stronghold on the Mississippi River and it was assured to fall into Union hands. As critical as Vicksburg was, President Lincoln and his Confederate counterpart, Jefferson Davis, knew all too well that events in the East were going to decide the outcome of the conflict.

General Robert E. Lee was not ready to sit idle and wait for the next Union thrust after Chancellorsville. He had communicated with Richmond for several months on his desire to make another invasion of the North and by late May saw an opportunity to take the initiative while Union forces appeared to be in disarray. Lee's objectives were quite simple: take the war out of Virginia so that the land could recover. He wanted to provide relief to farms and farmland devastated by battle and foraging armies, and to gather supplies for his hungry army. His army's movement north of the Potomac River would not only force the Union Army out of Virginia, but hopefully also draw Union troops away from the ongoing siege of Vicksburg. Once his army had raided northern territory, he could gather his troops for battle in an area to his liking. Politically, Lee reasoned a conclusive victory on northern soil would add weight to the growing Northern peace movement, apply pressure to the Lincoln administration to end the war and sue for peace, and provide sufficient reason for official recognition of the Confederacy by European powers. Lee's argument was reasonable to Jefferson Davis and though the Confederate president was nervous about Richmond not being fully protected, he approved the plan.

Confederate General Robert E. Lee. (LOC)

For Lee's men who had been living for months on reduced rations, Maryland and Pennsylvania were bursting with plenty. "I can hardly believe that a rebel army has actually left poor Virginia for a season," wrote Major Eugene Blackford of the 5th Alabama Infantry. "Of course there is no end of milk and butter which our soldiers enjoy hugely."

The slow pursuit of Lee by the *Army of the Potomac* not only alarmed War Department officials but shocked governors of northern states who clamored for something to be done to stop the rebel invasion. Political pressure on the Lincoln administration added to the tug of war between General Hooker and the U.S. War Department, which finally ended on June 28 as the *Army of the Potomac* concentrated at Frederick, Maryland. Completely frustrated by the mistrust and lack of support from War Department officials, General Hooker requested to be relieved of command, which was quickly granted.

Major General George Gordon Meade was ordered to take command of the army. "I have been tried and condemned," the surprised general remarked after receiving word of his appointment. Using traces of information known on Lee's whereabouts and objectives, Meade decided to send the army north to feel for the enemy and draw Lee into battle. The very next day, the *Army of the Potomac* marched out of their camps to search for the Confederates in Pennsylvania.

The Opening Shots

On June 30, Confederate troops left their camps at Cashtown and marched toward Gettysburg in search of supplies. Upon reaching the edge of Gettysburg, scouts spied a column of Union cavalry south of town, closing fast. Under orders not to initiate a battle, the Confederates

Union General George Gordon Meade. (LOC)

returned to Cashtown where they reported the encounter to their commander, Lt. General A.P. Hill. Hill agreed to send two divisions of his corps toward Gettysburg the next day to investigate the arrival of the mystery cavalrymen and the stage was set for the opening of the battle on July 1, 1863.

July 1, 1863 — The Battle Begins

The battle began early on the morning of July 1, when a Confederate column under General Henry Heth, marching east from Cashtown, encountered Union pickets three miles west of Gettysburg. Opponents sparred over the gently rolling farmland west of Gettysburg, until the cavalrymen were forced back to McPherson's Ridge

where Union infantry were just then arriving at 10 AM. The attacks and counterattacks that followed lasted until noon.

A brief noon-time lull gave commanders on both sides time to plan and augment their battle lines. The battle was renewed at 2 PM when Confederate forces attacked McPherson's Ridge and Oak Ridge. Union troops fought desperately, repulsing the attacks with heavy losses to both sides. General Lee arrived on the battlefield and though a battle had been initiated against his orders, he immediately saw an opportunity. Lee allowed the attack to continue knowing that the battered Union line would be pressured from three directions as soon as all of his troops had concentrated. After two hours of desperate fighting it was apparent to General Abner Doubleday, commanding the First Corps after the death of Reynolds, that none of the ridges west of Gettysburg could be held. He ordered a fighting withdrawal to Seminary Ridge. North of Gettysburg, the Eleventh Corps was in a predicament with too few troops to defend a large area. The Union line finally collapsed and thousands of Union soldiers pushed headlong through the streets, yards and alleys of Gettysburg, many taking refuge in outbuildings and churches already filled with the wounded and dying. Terrified citizens fled to their cellars while others risked their lives to help the injured. Those who could find their way to Cemetery Hill were met by General Winfield S. Hancock, sent to Gettysburg by General Meade, and reorganized into a line of defense from Cemetery Ridge to Culp's Hill. General Lee commanded General Ewell to continue his attack south of Gettysburg "if practicable." Unable to consolidate his forces before nightfall and with the threat of a large Union force on his left, Ewell deferred. The sounds of battle slowed to a murmur as night fell. Exhausted soldiers of both

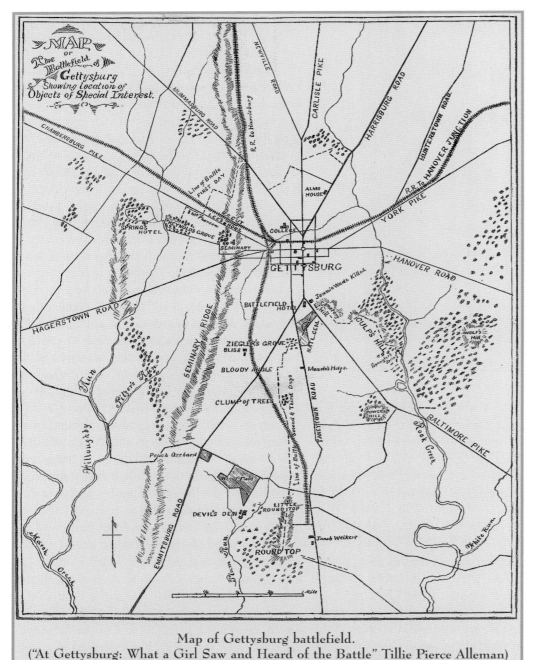

Map of Gettysburg battlefield.
("At Gettysburg: What a Girl Saw and Heard of the Battle" Tillie Pierce Alleman)

armies collapsed beside stone walls and fences, in fields and woods, and streets and alleys to wait for the fighting to resume on the morrow.

The southern victory of July 1 was not a decisive one. General Lee took the initiative to attack the following day, July 2, 1863, which would be the bloodiest day of the battle.

July 2, 1863 — The Bloodiest Day of the Battle

By the morning of July 2, the Union army had established strong positions along a giant U-shaped line from Culp's Hill to Cemetery Ridge. Satisfied with this position, General Meade decided to wait while the remainder of the *Army of the Potomac* hurried to the battlefield. From Seminary Ridge, General Lee studied the distant Union position. Simultaneous attacks on both the right and left flanks could roll up the Union line toward Cemetery Hill. Lee directed General A.P. Hill to continue to hold the Confederate center while General James Longstreet's Corps would attack the Union left and General Ewell's Corps would attack the right. Both had to strike at the same time to throw the Union off balance, not giving Meade time to shift troops to the threatened areas.

Major General Daniel E. Sickles, commander of the Third Army Corps, was unhappy with the location assigned him on the left flank. Finding that Confederates were massed on Seminary Ridge almost a mile in his front, Sickles ordered his corps to advance away from the main Union line and occupy high ground on the Emmitsburg Road. In doing so, Sickles made Meade's established line vulnerable. Meanwhile, General Longstreet's column reached the southern tip of Seminary Ridge at 3:30 PM after an exhausting 18-mile march. The Confederates deployed along the ridge and the men had only a few moments to rest and search for water before they were called into line and the attack began.

At 4 PM, Confederate cannoneers opened fire on Sickles' line. Fighting erupted at Devil's Den, in the Wheatfield, at the Peach Orchard, and on the slopes of Little Round Top. At approximately 6:30, General McLaws sent forward his Mississippi brigade for one last push. The Mississippi attack rammed through Union regiments near the Peach Or-

Big and Little Round Top, 1863. (LOC)

Fighting on Culp's & Cemetery Hills

In cooperation with Longstreet's attack on the Union left, General Ewell opened his cannonade on the Union right flank at 4 PM, but an overwhelming response of Union artillery from Cemetery Hill delayed the infantry assault. Confederate infantrymen under General Edward Johnson, after struggling against the terrain to get into position, were struck by deadly Union rifle fire delivered by a single brigade of New York troops under Brig. General George S. Greene. Johnson's men scattered for cover. Confused by the Union defense and believing that he was heavily outnumbered, Johnson decided to halt his attack, to wait for reinforcements, and renew his assault the next morning.

Northwest of Culp's Hill, two Confederate brigades under General Jubal Early momentarily penetrated the Union defenses at Cemetery Hill. Union reinforcements rushed to the scene and immediately attacked throwing the Confederates off Cemetery Hill for good.

Union troops of the Twelfth Army Corps that had pulled away from Culp's Hill on July 2, returned the following morning and attacked Johnson's troops. From the summit of the hill to the meadow near Spangler's Spring, combatants kept up a constant stream of rifle fire. Unable to break the Union stranglehold on Culp's Hill, Johnson finally withdrew after six hours of continuous fighting leaving the slopes covered with dead and wounded. By 11 AM on July 3, the southern threat at Culp's Hill had ended.

Late into the night, both army commanders evaluated the results of a long and brutal day. Apart from the precious foothold on Culp's Hill, the Confederate gamble of simultaneous attacks had failed. Lee was working at his headquarters

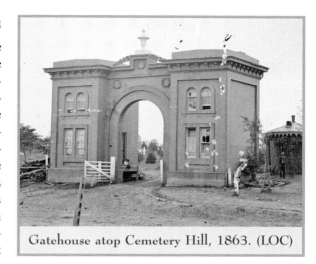
Gatehouse atop Cemetery Hill, 1863. (LOC)

chard and other Confederate units rushed from Seminary Ridge to exploit the break. The battered Union line wavered and slowly collapsed under the relentless Confederate pressure. Here the southerners found themselves at the doorway of a sizeable gap in the Union line between Cemetery Hill and Little Round Top, held by a handful of Union artillerymen and one regiment of foot soldiers, the 1st Minnesota Infantry. The Minnesotans charged into the Confederates and succeeded in slowing their attack, but at a terrible cost. Union reinforcements arrived and drove the Confederates back, but not before they had threatened the Union line right up to its center.

Darkness put a grateful end to the slaughter and Meade used the lull to shore up the left with fresh troops. By 10 PM, the line had been reestablished on Cemetery Ridge and extended to Big Round Top, where Union troops built stone barricades up to its summit. Exhausted soldiers reformed behind stone walls and laid down for the evening.

knowing that he could not sustain more than another full day of battle. When a delinquent General "JEB" Stuart arrived, Lee briefed him on the role of the cavalry for the next day. Meanwhile, General Meade held a "Council of War" at his headquarters on the Taneytown Road. Though the Union line had been restored by midnight there was still a sizeable Confederate force on Culp's Hill. Almost to a man, his generals agreed to stay at Gettysburg, retake and secure Culp's Hill, and then wait for Lee to attack. If he did not, then Meade should order a counterattack and force Lee to fight or flee. The Gettysburg Campaign was about to reach its climax.

July 3 — The Most Memorable Charge of the War

With the loss of his advantage at Culp's Hill, Lee decided to alter his strategy. Having already ordered his cavalry chief, "JEB" Stuart, to ride around the Union position and attack the Union supply line, Lee decided to strike what

The Round Tops as depicted in the *Battle of Gettysburg* cyclorama.

he thought to be a weakened Union center on Cemetery Ridge where he observed few troops and only a handful of batteries. If this section of Meade's line collapsed, it would threaten the Union rear and those strong hill positions. He issued orders for a massive bombardment aimed at this area followed by an assault of 12,000 men, coordinated and commanded by his trusted corps commander General James Longstreet. Longstreet's Assault, better known today as "Pickett's Charge," would be Lee's last gamble at Gettysburg.

At 1 PM, two guns stationed in the Peach Orchard fired the signal to begin the bombardment. Over 120 Confederate guns on Seminary Ridge simultaneously exploded, sending shot and shell toward Cemetery Ridge. Startled Union artillerymen sprang to their guns and soon both ridges were covered with thick, acrid smoke. The pounding of the guns in the great duel shook the earth for nearly an hour, when the Union fire finally slackened. Longstreet reluctantly gave the order for the infantry to advance and nearly 12,000 Confederate soldiers began the long march toward the Union line. Suddenly the Union artillery came back to life, blasting the formations and cutting large swaths

through them. As they reached the Emmitsburg Road, they were startled by the blast from hundreds of Union muskets. Officers were replaced by captains and sergeants, urging the men on until they reached "the Angle." Brig. General Lewis Armistead, the lone unscathed general of Pickett's Division, pierced the Union center, crossing the stonewall with about 300 men who raced into the remains of a Union battery and nearby grove of young trees, shrubs, and vines. This was the "High Water Mark" of the battle and, for the Confederacy, of the war.

North of the Angle, troops under Generals Pettigrew and Trimble reached the Emmitsburg Road to attack the Union line between Pickett's command and Ziegler's Grove only to meet a solid wall of musketry and artillery. Groups of Confederates leapt the fences and forged ahead, the size of each melting away as they surged up the slope toward the terrible stonewall that literally boiled with fire and smoke. None would pierce the Union line in this area. All along the line the attack ground to a halt and those who were able, turned back to Seminary Ridge. Pickett's Charge had failed.

General Meade rode onto the scene just as the last shots died away. A staff officer approached and informed the general that the southerners had been whipped. His army had done the unthinkable- beaten Robert E. Lee and the best troops he could throw at them. The tired general managed to utter a hoarse "Hurrah!", and then rode on to inspect the line.

General Lee witnessed the southern tide crest. Afterward, he spoke with the survivors, calming them with words of encouragement and preparing them for the Union counterattack that was sure to come. Within the hour, a courier informed Lee of "JEB" Stuart's defeat three miles east of Gettysburg at what is known today as East Cavalry Field. By no means did the Battle of Gettysburg decide the final outcome of the American Civil War, but it was one of the more decisive victories for the Union *Army of the Potomac* and came at a time where northern support for the Union cause was wavering. It was a turning point in the fortunes of the Confederacy — never again would Lee's *Army of Northern Virginia* be able to strike so far into the North or seriously threaten the northern capitol. Gettysburg was the beginning of the final path, which led these armies to the war's bloody close at Appomattox Court House, Virginia, on April 9, 1865.

For the complete virtual tour, please visit: *http://www.nps.gov/archive/gett/getttour/main-ms.htm*

CHAPTER 2

Cyclorama — More Than Just a Large Painting

Panorama is derived from the Greek words *pan* meaning "all" and *horama* meaning "view, sight" and generally describes a wide uninterrupted view of a scene or physical space. A cyclorama is a panoramic painting viewed in the round. Such a design allows the viewer, located on a central platform, a 360-degree view of the painting. In Europe, most round paintings were referred to as panoramas, but in America the term cyclorama was more commonly used.

The original 1787 patent for a cyclorama painting was held by Irish artist Robert Barker who conceived the idea to exhibit a painting without boundaries which would draw the viewer into the landscape. His cyclorama depicted a view of Edinburgh, Scotland. Tradition holds that Barker's inspiration came to him as he was climbing a hill in Edinburgh and, upon reaching the top, was awestruck at the view of the city below and around him. He devised a way to capture the scene on canvas. Many more cycloramas were painted for major cities in Europe before the genre came to America in the late 1870s. Subject matter included scenic landscapes, great works of literature, religious themes and epic historical events. Civil War battles were the most popular topic for American cycloramas. At a time when world travel was a luxury available only to the wealthy, cycloramas provided a mass medium to bring these scenes and events to the largest possible audiences.

Cycloramas were massive artistic achievements which traditionally measured 50 feet high and 400 feet in circumference, but they were a technical phenomenon as well. An artist painting a large landscape on a flat surface was limited only by the size of available canvas. However, painting that large landscape on a circular surface required some sophisticated adjustments in perspective; otherwise there would be considerable distortion to linear elements in the composition. As the medium of cyclorama painting evolved, the method was refined until the perfect illusion was achieved, an illusion described as "so true to life that it could be confused with reality." (The Painted Panorama, 1999, p.7)

The creation of the aforementioned illusion required that a number of physical features be in place (see diagram). The building itself, called a rotunda, was specifically designed in size and shape to complement the viewing of the cyclorama painting. The roof was fitted with a series of small glass panes near its outer edges

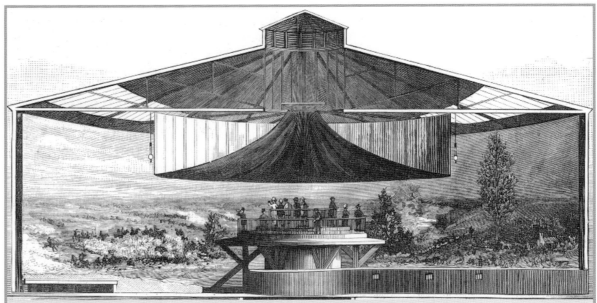

Diagram showing all of the elements necessary for a cyclorama exhibition. (*Scientific American*)

to allow sunlight to filter down onto the upper portion of the canvas just as natural daylight would illuminate the actual outdoor landscape. The painting was hung from a circular pipe near the ceiling but did not touch the floor. A second circular pipe was inserted into a wide hem at the bottom edge of the painting from which weights were suspended. This hanging system caused the center weave of the painting to bow inward creating a hyperbolic shape, with the center of the painting situated about a foot closer to the viewer than the top or bottom. This peculiar shape allowed the artist to layer the landscape in such a way as to give it the appearance of stretching out for many miles.

The viewing platform was situated in the center of the room, about thirty feet off the ground and forty feet from the painting in all directions. A draping light-colored canopy hung down from the center of the ceiling with its widest part above the platform just high enough to prevent the viewer from seeing the upper edge of the painting and roof structures above. By blocking these structural intrusions, the illusion was more easily obtained. The canopy also served to limit the amount of daylight from above.

A diorama, or three-dimensional landscape, filled the space between the bottom edge of the painting and the viewing platform, thereby extending certain terrain features. Fence lines and roads, began in the painting and continued into the foreground with real rocks, rails and rutted dirt, helped to complete the illusion.

By blurring all boundaries between the real and created worlds, the viewer experienced a sense of immersion when he climbed the dimly lit stairs and stepped into the center of the scene.

There were a number of steps necessary in preparation for the execution of a great cyclorama.

1. Subject

After selecting a subject for a battle cyclorama, the lead artist set out to obtain as much detailed information as possible about the event and its physical setting. He visited the field, made sketches, studied maps, interviewed participants and photographed the terrain. His preparation often took more than six months to complete.

2. Drafts

Upon retuning to his studio, the lead artist prepared a first plan or 'study' of the cyclorama. This smaller version was done at a 1:10 scale making it approximately 40 feet by 5 feet in size. When finished, the full-color study in oil or watercolor represented a detailed miniature of the finished cyclorama including the buildings, roads, fences and the placement of the military

An original pen and ink drawing for the *Battle of Atlanta* Cyclorama showing the grid lines. (Atlanta History Center)

units and their implements of war. The study was then traced onto paper of equal size, using pen and ink. A grid was drawn over the pen and ink sketch dividing it into ten sections, with sections then further divided into equal-sized blocks. Each block was designated by a letter representing the section and also by a number. This was done to aid the artists in enlarging the drawing and transferring it to the blank canvas which was also divided into an equal number of sections and blocks. Thus each square on the canvas was exactly ten times larger than those on the working drawing.

3. Canvas Preparation

A large canvas, approximately 50 feet by 400 feet, was carefully stretched and hung in the circular studio. The linen, somewhat heavier than that used for smaller paintings, was specially woven in Belgium in sections 30 feet wide. These sections were neatly stitched together before being shipped to the cyclorama studio. Upon arrival, the canvas was nailed to a large circular beam by riggers who often sang as they hauled it up and shook out the great folds. The lower ring was attached to the lower edge and weights were hung to achieve the stretch and shape necessary for the creation of the painted illusion.

4. Erecting the Scaffolds

After hanging the canvas, iron rails were laid on the floor, upon which movable scaffolds of different heights were placed. These were in fact rolling wooden towers, from ten and fifty feet in height, composed of a number of platforms which were reached by stairs. This arrangement enabled all members of the artistic team to reach all parts of the great canvas. Six of these cars were necessary to paint one cyclorama.

Diagram showing the scaffold towers used by artists to reach the cyclorama canvas.
(*Scientific American*)

5. Priming the Canvas

Next, the canvas was 'sized' with a solution of watered-down glue and then primed with a ton or more of 'whiting'. The treated canvas formed the surface upon which the artists painted, in colorful detail, the final work.

6. Transfer of the Image

Meanwhile, each section of the original pen and ink drawing was photographed onto glass plates. Several sets of prints were made to guide the team of artists. Then the glass plates, by means of several lenses and strong light, were used to project an enlarged image onto the primed canvas which, as mentioned before, was similarly lined off into sections and squares. In this manner, the original drawing was magnified and copied into the corresponding squares of the primed canvas. Because the canvas was so much larger than the drawing, the projected image seemed to contain too few figures, so many more figures were added to the scene. Civil War veterans were sometimes asked to pose in various attitudes with their soldier gear as they were sketched into the landscape.

7. Painting the Cyclorama

The lead artist supervised the work of the team, with each member lending his special talent to the process. There were artists who only painted horses, others who created military figures, one who only painted faces on the figures painted by someone else. There were usually two or more landscape artists and at least two who worked only on the sky portions of the painting. It was not unusual for one artist to paint the figure of a mounted officer and then move away so another artist could fill in the face. A third artist rapidly painted the horse under the soldier figure. Most of the artists who worked on American cycloramas were European immigrants, predominately of German and French descent. Many of them remained in America and sought other work after the cyclorama craze had passed. It was not uncommon to find them painting backdrops for theater productions in opera houses.

Paints were of high quality oil, comprised of natural pigments. One of the most expensive was the rich yellow color known as cadmium but was in fact cadmium sulfide. In the 1880s it cost about $50 for enough to fill a peach can. Cadmium selenide was a bright red pigment. The combination of the two cadmiums produced the orange pigment. Brown paints were umbers derived from iron oxide while some of the green pigments were copper arsenate derivatives.

A central platform, of the same size and height as the exhibition rotunda's viewing platform, was a staple of the cyclorama studio so that artists were able to periodically observe the effect and progress of their work. It was also a place for collaboration and conference among the members of the artistic team. Just as often, it was populated with veterans who came to admire and critique. Some of them had taken part in the scenes represented on the canvas and made helpful suggestions to correct or complete the artists' notes. For the most part, Civil War cycloramas provided well-documented visual history for those who viewed them.

8. Transporting the Canvas

When the painting neared completion, carpenters began to build a huge spool upon which to roll the canvas, and an equally huge crate to contain it for transportation to an exhibition site. The highest tower used to paint the canvas was cleared of artist's paraphernalia and converted to hold the spool upright. The weights and lower ring were removed from the canvas and one seam of the painting was opened. The edge of the canvas was nailed to the spool and as the canvas was loosened from the top ring, it was slowly and steadily rolled onto the upright spool. If all went as planned, in two hours the huge painting was rolled onto the spool. A cable was passed through the spool and used to lower the six or seven ton cyclorama into a shipping crate. Shipping was by rail on flat platform cars. Upon arrival at its destination, a track system resembling the one in the studio was quickly installed to facilitate installation in the exhibition rotunda.

9. Assembling the Illusion

While awaiting the arrival of the painting, men employed by the artist prepared the material for the diorama or artificial foreground and constructed the platform upon which it was to be built. This was done by following the ir-

The huge wooden rollers on which the finished canvas was rolled for transportation to an exhibition building. *(Scientific American)*

regular contours shown on the original cyclorama drawings. It is interesting to note that the lumber used for the diorama platform was treated with a silicate compound to keep moisture out and make it fire-proof. This would have been of significant importance since the trees, bushes, and grass used in the foreground were living but soon died, making them particularly flammable.

Hundreds of loads of earth were carted into the rotunda, along with fence rails, sod, logs and sand. A variety of battle equipage and debris were gathered to await their skillful distribution on the battleground. After the painting was installed, the foreground elements were so artfully arranged that they joined with the painting to appear as one landscape. Accounts from spectators relate that it was nearly impossible to determine at any point which part was real and which was the painted scene.

Authors' Note: The previous "steps to creating a cyclorama" were assembled from information found in two articles that appeared in 1886:

Davis, Theodore R. "How a Great Battle Panorama is Made." *St. Nicholas: An Illustrated Magazine,* Volume XIV; Part I, November 1886 to April 1887; pages 99-112, and *Scientific American, Volume LV, Number 19; November 6, 1886; page 296.*

Theodore R. Davis was an artist-correspondent during the Civil War who, because he traveled with Sherman's Army, was consulted by the artist creating the Atlanta Cyclorama.

The article in *Scientific American* described the making of a *Battle of Gettysburg* Cyclorama.

The diverse types of magazines in which these articles appeared demonstrate to the reader that cycloramas were indeed both artistic and technologic endeavors.

Cycloramas were displayed in Europe from the time of their invention in the late 1700s, but they enjoyed their greatest popularity in the late 1800s. It was then that the cyclorama craze hit America.

As noted earlier, the subject of most cycloramas included scenic landscapes, great works of literature and epic historical events, most often with religious or military themes. It was the Civil War of 1861-1865 that provided inspiration for most cyclorama paintings exhibited throughout America. With the overwhelming success of Paul Philippoteaux's first two *Battle of Gettysburg* Cycloramas produced in Europe in 1883-1884 for Chicago and Boston, several cyclorama studios opened in American cities. William Wehner operated a studio in Milwaukee, Wisconsin. His first painting was *Storming of Missionary Ridge* (1885-86), followed by *The Battle of Atlanta (*which has been on permanent exhibit in Atlanta since 1892). This company also had studios in Minneapolis, Chicago and Indianapolis.

Another cyclorama studio was managed by Pierpoint and Gross (later Gross and Reed) and was located in Englewood, Illinois (now part of Chicago). In addition to the *Chicago Fire* Cyclorama and *Jerusalem on the day of the Crucifixion*, this studio produced a number of battle paintings.

Several major Civil War battles were represented among these American cycloramas. In addition to the *Battle of Gettysburg* paintings, other cycloramas depicting *The Battle of Manassas or Second Bull Run, Battle of Shiloh, Lookout Mountain or the Battle above the Clouds, The Battle of Vicksburg* and even the naval engagement between the Monitor and Merrimac were produced.

However, Philippoteaux's *Battle of Gettysburg* Cycloramas were the first and remained the most popular by far. He eventually created four versions of his *Battle of Gettysburg* (which originally hung in Chicago, Boston, Philadelphia and Brooklyn, respectively) but other studios copied his work as well. These copies were known as "buckeyes," and the studio proprietors who produced them were not required to pay the original artists for the privilege of copying their work.

Incredibly, it was not too difficult to pirate a cyclorama. Souvenir photographs were often taken by local photographers and sold to visitors at the exhibitions. In the case of Philippoteaux's original *Battle of Gettysburg*, a series of images taken by H. H. Bennett of Chicago in 1884 were produced and sold as stereoviews. This format, which allowed the viewer to see the image in 3D, greatly enhanced the ability to see the layers of landscape unique to cyclorama paintings and made it easier to reproduce them. Boston photographers Allen & Rowell took a similar series of photos of Philippoteaux's second *Battle of Gettysburg*.

With a set of souvenir images and notes on paint colors obtained during a visit to an exhibition platform, a studio proprietor had all the information he needed to pirate a popular cyclorama.

Some of the buckeyes were of poor quality and would not be mistaken for the originals. But some were well done and were occasionally passed off as the originals by their promoters. An article in the October 1, 1886, Chicago *Herald* describing the cyclorama industry claimed that there were at least a dozen copies of the *Battle of Gettysburg* Cyclorama and possibly as many as two dozen. There were buckeyes of a few other cycloramas as well.

Some of the better *Gettysburg* buckeyes may have been created using Philippoteaux's original sketches in the hands of artists who had formerly worked for him but had moved on, taking their copies of the working drawings with them. Artist Marion Knight worked on at least one of Philippoteaux's Gettysburg cycloramas and later worked for the studio of Pierpoint and Gross. This company installed a permanent *Battle of Gettysburg* Cyclorama in Pittsburgh and also one at the Old Soldiers' Home in Dayton, Ohio. Both of these were later destroyed by fire. They also produced one or more *Gettysburgs* that traveled to various American cities beginning in 1886. A few years later, under the name Gross and Reed, the company exhibited a *Gettysburg* in Melbourne and Sydney, Australia from 1889 to 1906.

The Wehner studio may have produced a *Battle of Gettysburg* as early as 1886. Many of

MANUAL OF PANORAMA OF BATTLE OF SHILOH, CHICAGO.

GEN. GRANT AND STAFF.

"The battle still continued without cessation, our forces being gradually forced back at all points, though fighting heroically. Two hours rolled around, and no news from Gen. Lew Wallace, when, at 2:30 P.M. Gen. Grant directed me to go in search of him, report to him how matters stood, and hasten him forward. I asked Capt. Hawkins to accompany me." etc., etc.—REPORT OF LIEUT.-COL. AFTER...

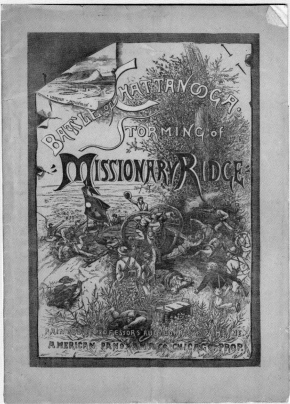

(Clockwise from top left) Cover of souvenir program for *Battle of Shiloh;* Section of the *Battle of Shiloh* cyclorama; Cover for *Missionary Ridge* souvenir program; Section of *Missionary Ridge* cyclorama; H. H. Bennett stereoview depicting a scene from the Chicago version of the *Gettysburg* cyclorama.

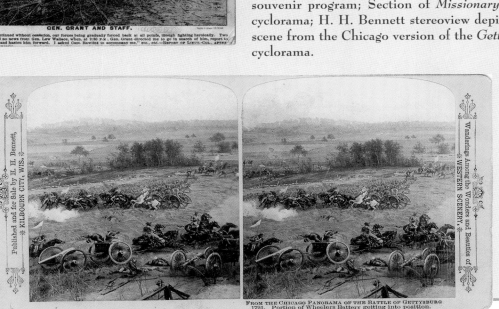

Published and for sale by H. H. Bennett, KILBOURN CITY, WIS.

Wanderings Among the Wonders and Beauties of WESTERN SCENERY.

FROM THE CHICAGO PANORAMA OF THE BATTLE OF GETTYSBURG
1721. Portion of Wheelers Battery getting into position.

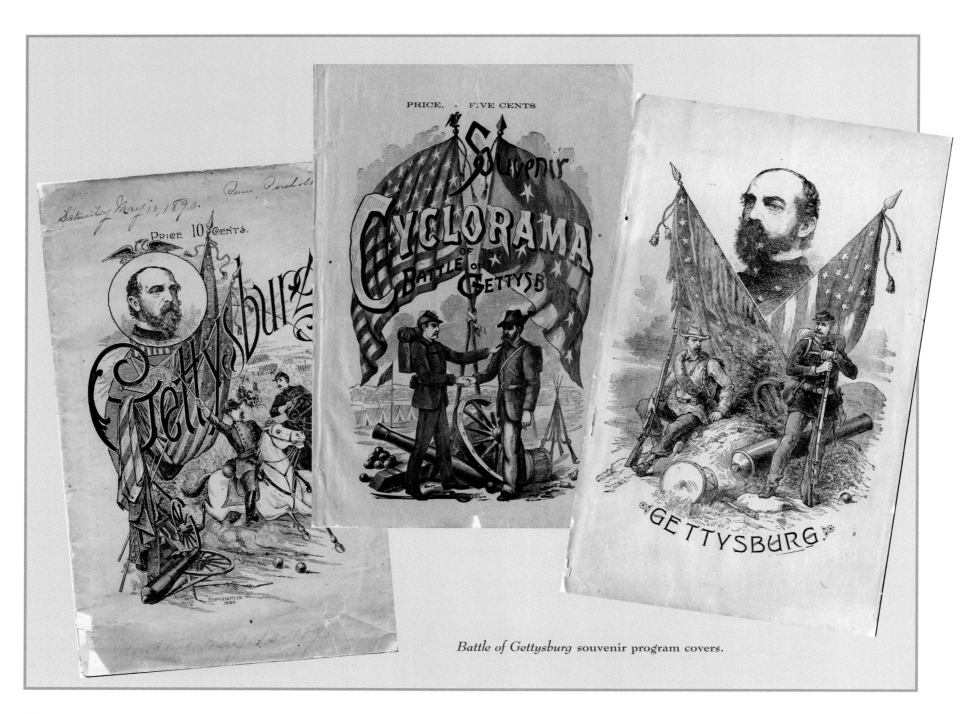

Battle of Gettysburg souvenir program covers.

Covers of the *Battle of Vicksburg* and *Battle of Manassas* (2nd Bull Run) souvenir programs.

Souvenir program cover for the *Battle of Gettysburg* shown in Melbourne, Australia.

Wehner's cycloramas were exhibited by promoter E. W. McConnell who claimed to have owned thirty cycloramas during his career. McConnell exhibited a *Gettysburg* Cyclorama at the Columbian Expo of 1893, again at the St. Louis Expo in 1904, the Century of Progress in Chicago in 1933 and the Texas Centennial Expo in 1936.

English artist E. J. Austen worked on a number of cycloramas with Philippoteaux and later in a Chicago studio. It is the opinion of retired National Park Service historian Don Johnson, and of author Sue Boardman, that Austen painted the *Battle of Gettysburg* Cyclorama which was stored at Wake Forest University from 1965 until it was sold to investors in 2007. This was the same *Gettysburg* Cyclorama exhibited in Chicago in 1933 by McConnell which may have led to the current misconception that it was the original 1883 Chicago *Battle of Gettysburg* painted by Philippoteaux. Comparison of extant photographs of Philippoteaux's Chicago *Battle of Gettysburg* and McConnell's Chicago *Gettysburg* prove conclusively that these are two similar but distinctly different paintings.

Preliminary research suggests that there may have been as many as fifty or more cycloramas circulating in America around 1890, including originals and buckeyes.

So what happened to them?

In the early years of cyclorama exhibition, paintings were installed in specially built rotundas in some of the larger American cities, each painting remaining in its intended location for months or even years. Sophisticated urbanites of the middle and upper classes were the primary consumers during this time. But as the cyclorama phenomenon evolved, exhibitions quickly became highly commercialized entertainment for the masses. Consequently, cyclorama exhibition became more of a money-making endeavor and less of an artistic one. For example, the first two versions of Philippoteaux's *Battle of Gettysburg* remained in their initial rotundas in Chicago and Boston for more than six years. The last two versions, made for Philadelphia and Brooklyn, remained in their respective locations for just one year before moving on to other locations. By the late 1890s and beyond, some cycloramas were shown for just a few weeks or months, housed in temporary buildings and large tents. Expos and state fairs were particularly popular later settings.

As the exhibition structures became less permanent and venues became more varied and of shorter duration, dramatic light and sound shows began to accompany the paintings, along with cluttered dioramas filled with wax or cardboard figures dressed as wounded and dead soldiers. These conditions increased the potential for destruction by fire. Constant setting up and tearing down took a toll on the large canvases, as did the loading and unloading of the rolled paintings onto and off of railroad cars. Many cycloramas simply disintegrated, while others were lost to water damage or extreme weather. The *Missionary Ridge* Cyclorama was destroyed in a tornado that collapsed the exhibition building. Another tornado in Sioux City, Iowa destroyed a *Gettysburg* Cyclorama in 1894. A hail storm broke most of the glass panes in the rotunda roof in St. Paul, Minnesota in 1887 exposing that cyclorama to heavy rain. Some of these massive paintings were cut into smaller scenes, framed, and given to people and groups who had a connection to the painting. In one case

there is evidence that a cyclorama was dismantled to make tents on an Indian Reservation.

According to Harry Lichter, Curator of Collections at the State Historical Society of Wisconsin, in a letter to Gettysburg National Park historian Alfred Mongin (dated June 10, 1953; NPS Archives): "One of the Milwaukee Gettysburg Panoramas was bought by the Japanese government before the Russo-Japanese war. It was taken to Tokyo and used to teach tactics to the officer cadets." He cited the *Milwaukee Journal*, October 2, 1921, as the source for this information. He went on to report: "A version painted by the Lohr group was destroyed in a fire. A Baron von Kotzhausen of Milwaukee bought it for reasons unknown. On the way to Milwaukee, it burned on a freight siding at Indianapolis...."

...Mr. Theodore Mueller, Curator of the Milwaukee County Historical Museum states that about 1949 he was informed that an old panorama of Gettysburg was stored in a vacant lot in an industrial section of Milwaukee.... On arriving at the lot he did find a crate about 40 feet long; he pried off some of the boards but was scared off by a horde of rats which emerged and by the filthy condition of the canvas."

Some were simply sold when they no longer made money. The following notice appeared in the *Brooklyn Eagle* theater section on March 3, 1889: "Among the things advertised for sale in amusement agencies are circus wagons, performing dogs, The Battle of Gettysburg cyclorama, a Pullman car and a demon child."

Still, it is mystifying that so many of these large canvasses were simply and inexplicably 'lost.'

One of the several 'buckeye' versions of the *Battle of Gettysburg* cyclorama. There may have been as many as 12 versions of this painting.

CHAPTER 4

The Gettysburg Cycloramas by Philippoteaux

The *Battle of Gettysburg* Cyclorama by French artist Paul Philippoteaux was the first of more than 50 Civil War battle paintings exhibited in America beginning in the 1880s. Its phenomenal success led the artist to produce three more versions and inspired several other studios to produce copies as well.

Paul Dominique Philippoteaux (1846-1923) was born in Paris and educated at the College Henri IV and at the Ecole des Beaux Arts in Paris. He also studied art in the studios of his father, Felix Philippoteaux, Leon Cogniet, and Alexander Cabanal. Philippoteaux made numerous sketches for Guizot's *History of France* and may be recognized by American readers for his illustrations contained in the works of Alexander Dumas and Jules Verne. He gained a reputation as an artist of other cyclorama paintings, including the *Crucifixion*, exhibited at St. Anne de Beaupre in Quebec, Canada. He was associated with his father in the production of the cyclorama of the *Siege of Paris*, originally exhibited in Paris and later in the Americas. It was the latter cyclorama that drew the attention of merchant and entrepreneur Charles L. Willoughby.

Charles Louis Willoughby was born in Hooksett, New Hampshire in 1838. He entered the retail business at a young age, first in Lowell, Massachusetts and later in New York and Ohio. In 1870 the firm of Willoughby and Hill was founded in Chicago and cleared $50,000 in its first year of business. Although Willoughby and his partner lost the store in the Chicago fire of 1871, they recovered quickly by obtaining goods from clothing brokers in New York which were sold from farms and sheds. By the 1880s, Charles was a wealthy merchant and entrepreneur. He commissioned Paul Philippoteaux to create a cyclorama for the

French artist Paul Philippoteaux, who created four *Battle of Gettysburg* cyclorama paintings.

sum of $50,000. Willoughby and Philippoteaux, along with several other investors, formed the National Panorama Company for the purpose of bringing the *Battle of Gettysburg* Cyclorama to Chicago. This was the first of several stock companies created to finance exhibitions in this and several other cities.

Having selected the climactic action of July 3, 1863 at Gettysburg as his subject, Philippoteaux began his preparatory work for the grand painting. It would be more than a year before it was unveiled to the public in October of 1883. In an interview published in the *New York Times* in May 1882, the artist remarked that he was in that city to call on General Hancock who had given him "a number of interesting details." He also spent some time sketching artifacts in the museum at Governor's Island and interviewing General Webb and General Doubleday. He travelled to Washington to study battle maps in the War Department files and spent several weeks in Gettysburg making detailed notes and sketches of the terrain. One of the earliest battlefield guides at Gettysburg, local Civil War veteran William Holtzworth, proudly reported in his memoir that he took the artist on an extensive battlefield tour. Under Philippoteaux's careful direction, noted battlefield photographer William H. Tipton produced a series of photographs of the landscape from a point near the copse of trees on Cemetery Ridge. These panoramic images were taken from a 30-foot high wooden platform, the same height as the plat-

(Left) William D. Holtzworth, Civil War veteran and early battlefield guide; accompanied Philippoteaux on the battlefield as he prepared to create the Gettysburg cyclorama.

(Right) William H. Tipton, battlefield photographer, produced a series of ten images from a position just behind the angle on Cemetery Ridge. These were used by Philippoteaux to create the landscape accurately in the painting.

form from which the painting would be viewed by spectators during the it's exhibition.

Armed with his research, Philippoteaux's next step was to produce a scaled-down version of the *Battle of Gettysburg* painting, a full-color study in oil.

The Chicago Version

Upon completing his preliminary studies, Philippoteaux left the United States for his studio in Brussels, Belgium, where he assembled his team and set to work. Various sources state that his team numbered between five and twenty artists, each with his own specialty. At least two landscape artists were employed, in addition to those

for whom horses, uniforms, portraits or sky fell within the scope of their special skills. Many of Philippoteaux's team were of German or French descent, and some of them continued to work with him on the other *Gettysburg* versions painted in France and the United States. Although the names of some of the artists who worked on one or more of the four versions are known, it is impossible to know exactly which artists worked on which paintings with two exceptions. In the descriptive brochure for Philippoteaux's cyclorama *Jerusalem on the Day of the Crucifixion,* it is stated that Parisian painters Salvador Mege and Ernest M. Gross worked with Philippoteaux on "all of his cycloramas which

have been seen in America." Others who worked on one or more *Battle of Gettysburg* cycloramas include Marion Knight; Englishman E. J. Austen; and American painters John H. Twachtman and John O. Anderson, both born in Cincinnati, Ohio. Some of these artists would go on to create other *Gettysburg* cycloramas after leaving Philippoteaux's employ.

Landscape artists were thought to carry the most skill in the creation of a cyclorama. A review of the *Battle of Gettysburg* painting in *L'Art Moderne* (Modern Art) magazine, published in Brussels in May 1883 remarked that "what really constitutes the highest beauty and is superior to anything seen up to this time is the landscape. The sky is of a prodigious clearness and truth. When one raises the eyes the illusion is marvelous..."

As the first version of the *Battle of Gettysburg* Cyclorama neared completion in Brussels, a special building known as a rotunda was being erected on the corner of Wabash Avenue and Hubbard Court in Chicago. Its unusual appearance drew comments in the press: "it is rare that any single amusement enterprise...projects and erects a large and substantial building for its own use, and especially one wholly unfit for any other use," said an article that appeared in the *Chicago Times* on December 2, 1883. *Chicago's Inter Ocean* newspaper reported that "in order to give this grand work its full effect, the artist has erected a fine fireproof duo-octagonal building...at a cost of $40,000, which is 134 feet in diameter and is 96 feet high. The walls are windowless, the light coming in only from the roof in daytime, while at night the building is brilliantly illuminated by electric light."

By November 1883, the National Panorama Company, the stock company formed by Charles

Willoughby and eight others, had formally purchased the painting from the artist for $200,000.

On the Saturday before opening the exhibition to the general public, the managers held a private preview and reception for prominent citizens and members of the press "who were not only charmed but astonished with what they saw....it only remains to be said that the universal verdict of those who have seen it is that the artist has rendered art in Chicago a great service in placing it on exhibition. The *Battle of Gettysburg* has at once taken a first position among the standard attractions of the city," as reported by the *Chicago Journal* on Decemmber 22, 1883.

The great success of Philippoteaux's painting became apparent almost immediately. The newspapers continued to give it high praise as visitors flocked to see it in the weeks and months that followed.

The *Chicago Times* reported on December 2, 1883, "The panorama of 'The Battle of Gettysburg' is universally conceded by all who have seen it, to be the most extraordinary work of art ever seen in this city. To describe it in words is impossible. It must be seen, in order to have any idea of its striking realistic effect."

The *Chicago Tribune* touted it as "a triumph of realistic painting" and the *Chicago Inter Ocean* commented that "the panorama, with its wonderful accessions, is certainly one of the most realistic and superb battle scenes ever shown in America. It has wonderful depths of perspective, strange plays in color, is splendid in action, and thoroughly replete with the rush and roar of battle."

A common interpretive method employed during exhibitions was to have a veteran lecture about what was represented in the painting. Many Civil War veterans flocked to see it, and to hear one of

The rotunda in Chicago where the first of Philippoteaux's *Battle of Gettysburg* paintings was exhibited starting in 1883.

their own speaking to and about them on the platform. In a July 1884 issue of *Frank Leslie's Illustrated Newspaper* a journalist remarked that "the enthusiasm of the old soldiers – and there were thousands of them – who gaze upon this panorama is unbounded." Many of them shared their approval of the painting with the artist, and a few criticized it for its historical inaccuracies. For example, in this first version, veterans remarked that some of the uniforms looked French, and that General Armistead was shown mounted on a horse although he crossed the field on foot that day.

Shortly after visiting the Cyclorama in mid-1884, General John Gibbon, a division commander of the Union Army's 2nd Corps, wrote to fellow officer Henry Hunt, chief of the Union artillery during the battle:

"Whilst in Chicago I went to see the battle of Gettysburg three times, and you may rest assured you have got a sight to see before you die. It is simply wonderful and I never before had an idea that the eye could be so deceived by paint and canvas.... You enter the building by a dark passageway and staircase and reach

a platform and the effect is startling for apparently you look out upon the field of Gettysburg from a point just behind the middle of my Div. The perspective and representation of the landscape is simply perfect and I say nothing more than the truth when I tell you it was difficult to disabuse my mind of the impression that I was actually on the ground. They tell a story of some rebel battery comdr. whose statement was disputed by some one declaring with an oath that if some one would get him a horse he would ride out there at once to the very place where his battery was! The whole field of Gettysburg with country for 15 or 20 miles back is around you. In any ordinary picture your view is limited by the frame, and were the top of the wall upon which the canvas is hung is concealed by a sort of umbrella suspended over your head with a drop around the edge like the fringe of a lady's parasol. In this way you look out on the perfectly painted sky and landscape with nothing whatever between you and the landscape. To farther deceive the eye the sloping space between the stand and bottom of the picture is made of ground in which grass and bushes are growing. Along the slope are scattered various natural objects — a hay stack full size, a piece of a stone wall, a gun, one wheel off, muskets, sabres knapsacks hats and etc.... You look right down on the struggle taking place in the angle of the stone wall in the middle of my Div. The men are fighting hand to hand, Cushing as he is falling at his piece is speaking to Webb on horse with drawn sword waving forward some approaching infantry and Hancock is close by, surrounded by his staff. A battery of arty. Is coming up at a gallop, and close by you are on an iron grey.... The scene is a very spirited one but not very true to fact and I do not like ex-

General John Gibbon, a division commander in the Union 2nd Corps at Gettysburg, saw the Chicago version and wrote to Chief of Artillery Henry Hunt encouraging him to see it. (LOC)

actly the way in which the artist has handled the military part of the picture. The attacking force is massed and larger than it was, extends to far to my left, and instead of representing the left of my Div. Coming up on the flank of the assaulting party they came up from the rear and men are represented as leaving the stone wall behind which they were posted and attacking from the right. But it's a wonderful picture and you ought to see it." (Original letter is a part of the Gilder-Lehrman Collection housed in the New York Historical Society.)

To mark the occasion of General Gibbon's visit, Emile Glogau, an early manager of the *Battle of Gettysburg* Cyclorama in Chicago, presented Gibbon with a souvenir folder containing images of the painting which he inscribed for the general. Austrian-born Glogau was an associate of Willoughby's in Chicago and may have been the person who introduced Willoughby to Philippoteaux in the early 1880s.

Visitors to the *Battle of Gettysburg* exhibition had the opportunity to purchase a souvenir program containing background information about the battle, a biography of the artist, a number of advertisements for local businesses and a fold-out key to the painting that aided the viewer to understand what he was seeing. Later issues of the program contained opinions of the press and listed names of Civil War veterans who visited the exhibition.

In a short time the *Battle of Gettysburg* became a popular and recognizable icon in Chicago and elsewhere. In 1885 and 1886, the Cyrus McCormick reaper, by then several decades old and widely accepted as the top mechanized farm tool on the market, used a scene from the *Battle of Gettysburg* Cyclorama in its advertisement entitled "Harvesting Interrupted." The harvester can be seen sitting in the field of wheat near General Hunt and his staff as the battle rages a few hundred yards away.

The painting remained in Chicago for three years and was then shown in Detroit in 1886. Newspaper advertisements indicate that it was later returned to its original location on Wabash and Hubbard Court where it competed with a buckye being shown at the 1893 Chicago World's Fair.

According to a letter written by the company that managed the painting, over two million people saw it in the first ten years it was on display, and its stockholders were paid $420,000 in dividends after expenses or about $25,000 per year for the first ten years it was exhibited.

After 1893, it is difficult to determine where the Chicago version was exhibited. By then there were a number of copies, made by other studios, circulating around the country. Photographic evidence does prove, however, that Phlippoteaux's original Chicago version is not the same painting shown in Chicago at the 1933 Century of Progress Expo which eventually ended up in storage at Wake Forest University.

The original Chicago rotunda was razed in 1940 to make room for office buildings.

The Boston Version

Within months of opening Chicago's cyclorama exhibition, Willoughby's commission for a second version of the *Battle of Gettysburg*, to be permanently located in Boston, was underway. For this commission, Philippoteaux took his team of artists to Paris, to a studio familiar to him and owned by the same company that owned the Brussels studio.

In April 1884, Willoughby made application to the inspector of buildings for the City of Boston to construct an exhibition building, offering a single word for its purpose: "Cyclorama."

The Boston painting opened in December 1884 and was again preceded by a special preview and reception of dignitaries and other prominent citizens. Although the rotunda at 541 Tremont Street and Philippoteaux's *Battle of Gettysburg* Cyclorama were new to Boston, Bostonians were already familiar with the art form and with the name Philippoteaux. Since 1878, the *Siege of Paris*, painted by Felix Philippoteaux assisted by his son Paul, was ex-

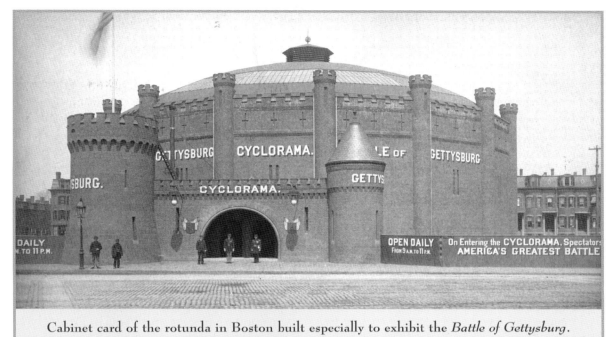
Cabinet card of the rotunda in Boston built especially to exhibit the *Battle of Gettysburg*.

hibited in a temporary iron building on Columbus Avenue and Ferdinand Street.

As in Chicago, the Boston version of the *Battle of Gettysburg* enjoyed great success.

The Sunday Herald gave it rave reviews in its coverage of the preview, stating, "Of the painting as a work of art, there is no dispute.... The figures are singularly life-like and animated; and in fact, the whole picture is full of action. It is difficult and in some places impossible to tell where the canvas leaves off and the artificial foreground begins. The atmosphere is simply marvelous in its fidelity to nature.... The painting draws forth that...particularly truthful remark that it must be seen to be fully appreciated."

On December 26th, *The Daily Advertiser* reported, "The new cyclorama of 'The Battle of Gettysburg'...is an important addition to the list of amusements in this city and possesses a still more important claim to interest as a work of art.... The execution of this truly colossal work is a marvel of artistic learning and sentiment, as well as of accuracy in every historical and topographical particular. In a word, this is a great piece of work.... The industry and system, the patience and fineness in the little things, and the breadth and spirit of the whole effect are very remarkable and admirable."

A week later, *The Daily Transcript* printed these comments: "Certainly a most extraordinary affair is this 'Battle of Gettysburg,' whether judged by itself as a piece of realistic painting, or by the result which it unmistakably attains. The bewildering impression which it produces upon the spectator may perhaps explain the very uncritical mood which the work creates."

The *Boston Journal* reported, "The perspective is perfect, and the trees, men, animals and all things stand out as though a vast expanse of country were stretching away from one's feet...Of the details of the picture it would be impossible to speak....The exhibition is one which will long be a source of pleasure to the people of Boston and vicinity, while those who visit it will return again and again, and which, as a local institution, cannot be regarded with other feelings than those of gratification."

On December 30, *The Sunday Globe* remarked that "You will find hard work to convince yourself that you are not standing on the top of Cemetery Ridge in the very center of the position occupied by the troops of the Northern army on that memorable day in July, nearly twenty-two years ago. Looking over the brow of the hill on which you are standing, you see spread out before you the battlefield so vivid and life-like."

As in Chicago, Civil War veterans were frequent visitors to the viewing platform and could often be heard discussing their battle experiences.

The souvenir program sold to visitors in Boston was similar in size and format to the one sold in Chicago and the key was identical even though the artist made a dramatic change in the scene looking due east. This scene in the Chicago painting showed several large straw stacks with many wounded soldiers lying about. General Meade's headquarters appears as a small white building on the east side of the Taneytown Road. For the Boston version, a large white building resembling Meade's headquarters is prominently placed where the largest of the straw stacks stood in the Chicago version. In addition, a stone well and a wooden lean-to were now shown where a surgeon and his assistant now cared for a wounded soldier. These changes are not reflected in the key, possibly because it was more cost efficient to use the original one.

The Boston version of the *Battle of Gettysburg* remained on permanent exhibition in that city until 1891, at which time it was contracted to Philadelphia for one year in exchange for a cyclorama of *General Custer's Last Fight*. From 1892 until about 1899, its whereabouts are unknown although, based on its poor condition when next exhibited (in 1910), it may have been shown in other, less professionally staged, venues. This is based on the fact that, when it was uncrated in 1910 after being stored for years on a vacant lot, it was found to have been cut horizontally into two sections so that the bottom portion was 27 feet high and the sky portion was 19 feet high. If the painting had been exhibited in Philadelphia for a year as mentioned above and then returned directly to Boston, it would have most likely still been intact since the Philadelphia rotunda would have accommodated the full-sized painting. In any case, sometime before 1899, it was on the vacant lot behind the Boston rotunda. Although a precise date for the arrival of the painting on the lot is not known, records indicate that the rotunda was sold in 1899 to the New England Electric Vehicle Transportation Company so it seems unlikely that the painting was sent back to that location after 1899 if the original cyclorama company no longer owned the property.

While on the vacant lot, the painting was rolled up and contained inside a wooden crate approximately 50 feet in length. The next mention of this painting is in the *Boston Globe* dated March 11, 1901, "The famous panorama of the Battle of Gettysburg...is going to rack and ruin in a lot at the corner of Clarendon Street and Warren Avenue....a tiny pitched roof extends over the box, but the weather has played sad havoc with both the roof and the box, and the probabilities are that the canvas is pretty well damaged, for it has been in this place for a number of years."

Meade's headquarters as depicted in the Gettysburg cyclorama. (Gettysburg Foundation)

View of the Chicago Gettysburg cyclorama looking east; the scene was changed to show Meade's headquarters in this location for the remaining three versions.

The *Boston Evening Telegraph* reported on March 14, 1901, that the box "....was surrounded by rubbish....the sleet and snow and sun and rain had beat upon it, warping the thin roofed boards and opening the knotholes and cracks for rain to soak in. Boys have torn away a board here and there, which has permitted further injury. The leaky, weather-beaten box is really a sort of mausoleum of greatness. It contains a painting that cost $100,000 and made fame for the painter and thousands of dollars for those who exploited the production."

Boston's *Evening Transcript* from March 16, 1901 added, "Interest in the great cycloramic painting, 'The Battle of Gettysburg,' has been revived through recent discovery that the great canvas, which once was viewed with admiration by thousands upon thousands of people, is now seemingly going to ruin because of the conditions under which it is stored in this city....where it has remained for five or six years, or perhaps even longer, subjected to all the conditions of weather." The article goes on, "it is said at the office of the George Frost Company, corner of Tremont and Clarendon Streets, that the storage box made its appearance upon this vacant lot in a somewhat mysterious way. The company's offices overlook the lot and one morning the clerks and others in the office discovered that during the previous night the box had been dumped behind the factory.....The long box has been on fire two or three times in the years it has lain in the lot. Early last summer was the latest incident of this kind, and at that time the firemen played the hose well all over the box and into it, boards having been removed from the top.....An oiled skin or cloth is wrapped about the canvas and in the box, stored with it, are muskets and other paraphernalia which, as many will recall, formed a part of the foreground...."

Cover of souvenir program for the *Battle of Gettysburg* cyclorama in Chicago.

Souvenir program for the Boston cyclorama.

The *Battle of Gettysburg* cyclorama painting remained on the vacant lot in Boston until 1910.

Stockholders in the Boston Cyclorama Company, which had taken financial control of the painting in 1885, dissolved in 1904.

Today, the Boston exhibition rotunda still exists but now stands behind a brick façade with only its roof visible from the street.

Additional details on this version of the painting and what happened to it after 1910, will be discussed in the next chapter.

The Boston rotunda currently houses the Boston Center for the Arts. (Suzanne Wray)

The Philadelphia Version

Philippoteaux created two more versions of his *Battle of Gettysburg* and both opened to the public in 1886. Philadelphia's cyclorama building stood at the corner of Broad and Cherry Streets where the painting opened in February 1886. This version most closely resembled the Boston version. In fact, the key to the Boston painting had not been updated to show the differences between it and the Chicago version so when Boston's painting came to Gettysburg for exhibition in 1913, the Philadelphia key was used.

A little over a year after it arrived in Philadelphia, the painting was moved to Cincinnati, Ohio.

Major Charles Hale, a veteran of the battle of Gettysburg, served as lecturer on the platform during exhibitions for at least the first three years of this painting's exhibitions. Hale was a veteran of the 5th New Hampshire Infantry which served during the battle, and was already known on the lecture circuit for his popular delineations on many battles of the war. As soon as the Philippoteaux *Battle of Gettysburg* Cyclorama opened, Hale became its main platform lecturer.

While the painting was being moved to Ohio, Hale spent many weeks at Gettysburg serving as a battlefield guide. A reunion between veterans of the Philadelphia Brigade and those of Pickett's Division was held during the first week of July 1887. During this reunion, Hale took many of his fellow veterans on tours around the field. A note written in his scrapbook (now in the Gettysburg National Military Park collection) states, "It was probably the greatest event that has taken place on the field since the battle was fought. The reminiscences of the survivors were graphic and interesting and Major Hale gained many good points." While in Gettysburg, he distributed a handbill advertising the reopening of the cyclorama painting in October and encouraged Ohio veterans who were in the battle to gather points of historical interest and incidents for use during his lectures in Cincinnati.

After a successful run in Cincinnati, including as a main attraction at the Ohio Centennial celebration in 1888, the painting was shown in St. Louis beginning in 1889. After that, this third version of Philippoteaux's *Battle of Gettysburg* was lost to history.

The Philadelphia rotunda on Broad and Cherry Streets. (NPS)

The rotunda in Cincinnati, circa 1887. (NPS)

(Above) Charles A. Hale, 5th New Hampshire Volunteers who fought in the Wheatfield at Gettysburg. (NPS)

(Top, right) Charles Hale in the 1880s when he served as lecturer for the Philadelphia version of the *Battle of Gettysburg* (NPS*)*

(Bottom, right) Hale's business card, listing him as a battlefield guide and cyclorama lecturer. (NPS)

(Center) Broadside distributed by Hale at Gettysburg to encourage Ohio veterans to share their personal stories. He would later use these reminiscences in his lectures from the cyclorama platform in Cincinnati. (NPS)

PHILIPPOTEAUX'S

GREAT MASTER PIECE,

THE

CYCLORAMA

OF THE

Battle of Gettysburg,

Shown in Philadelphia at Broad and Cherry Streets for the last two years, will open

In Cincinnati, O.,

EARLY IN OCTOBER.

Major Charles A. Hale, formerly of the 5th N. H. Regiment, who served on the staff of the 1st Brigade, 1st Division of the 2d Corps during the battle, and who lectured to nearly 250,000 people at the Cyclorama in Philadelphia, is now at Gettysburg, and will be pleased to meet Ohio Veterans who were in the battle, to gather points of historical interest and incidents for the lectures in Cincinnati.

The Cyclorama is now in the building especially adapted for it at Seventh and Elm Streets, Cincinnati. It was painted by Philippoteaux in Paris, brought over in 1865, and is unquestionably the finest historical battle scene in this country. Next year at Ohio's Centennial it will be one of the grandest attractions of that great occasion.

LATE 5TH N. H. V.
1ST BRIGADE.
1ST DIVISION.
2D CORPS.

Maj. Charles A. Hale,

BATTLEFIELD GUIDE AT GETTYSBURG;

LECTURER FOR PHILIPPOTEAUX'S CYCLORAMA OF THE BATTLE.

FOR THREE YEARS IN PHILADELPHIA AND CINCINNATI;

NOW MANAGER AND LECTURER WITH THE

P. O. ADDRESS,
BEVERLY, N. J.

GETTYSBURG EXHIBITION CO.

The New York Version

Philippoteaux's last *Battle of Gettysburg* painting opened on October 15, 1886, to an audience of invited guests who attended the sneak preview at the rotunda located at City Hall Square in Brooklyn. The *Brooklyn Eagle*, on October 2nd, reported, "When the Old Dutch Church property was purchased last spring and ground was broken for the new structure, few people had any conception of the magnitude of the enterprise. As the work progressed and the large iron structure gradually grew into shape....a better idea of what was to be was gained..... The canvas is the largest ever painted for a cyclorama. It is 50 feet wide and over 400 feet in length, presenting over 20,000 square feet of surface. It was painted by Mr. Philippoteaux and assistants at his big cylindrical studio on One Hundred and Forty Ninth Street, New York. It weighs over four tons and was delivered at the building rolled on a huge iron cylinder.....To transport it from the Harlem studio, one of the large trucks upon which the Brooklyn Bridge cars were delivered was used. To get it into place within the building required the work of twenty men for five days."

The *Brooklyn Eagle* covered the opening event in its October 16th edition:

"At 2 o'clock yesterday afternoon the doors of the building...were thrown open. The proprietors, Mr. Edward Brandus and Mons. Philippoteaux, ...issued a large number of personal invitations to city officials, members of the press and prominent society people...nearly 2,000 persons visited the exhibition between the hours of 2 and 5 P.M."

A number of influential officers were in attendance, including Generals Doubleday, Sickles, Slocum, Carr, and Graham (all veterans of the

Woodcut of the rotunda in Brooklyn where the last of Philippoteaux's Gettysburg cycloramas opened.

battle) and numerous commanders of the Grand Army veterans' posts of Brooklyn. The newspaper article went on to describe another veteran in attendance that day, "Captain John F. Chase, the battle scarred veteran, who has been retained as lecturer at the cyclorama, was arrayed in a neat uniform and delivered his description of the great painting in a very credible manner. It was his first appearance before the public as a speaker, but his heart was in his work and he described the points of the painting in an interesting and entertaining manner."

Captain Chase served in the Battle of Gettysburg with the 5th Maine Battery which was positioned on Steven's Knoll. On July 2nd, during the attack against Cemetery Hill, Chase received devastating wounds which cost him his right arm and left eye. He bore an additional 48 wounds from shrapnel and lay on the battlefield for two days before being picked up by a burial

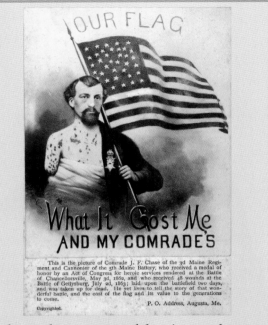

John F. Chase, veteran of the 5th Maine battery at Gettysburg where he received over 48 wounds on July 2nd. (NPS)

Chase as he appeared on the New York cyclorama platform. (NPS)

crew. His post-war business card shows him wearing the Medal of Honor he received for his heroic service in the Battle of Chancellorsville.

The newspapers made comparisons to previous cyclorama exhibitions in the city, including the *Battle of Vicksburg* and the *Monitor and Merrimac* and found the *Battle of Gettysburg* superior on many counts, especially citing the richness and color of the landscape and the illusion produced upon entering the platform. Some of the early press coverage included comments such as, "stirring battle scenes," "clever illusion," and "a master work."

Souvenir programs were available for purchase and contained much the same material as the ones representing the three previous versions, including the fold-out key to the painting.

Research indicates that this painting was not intended to be as permanent as the first three in their initial locations. Advertisements during the opening weeks of exhibition clearly state the cyclorama was to be in Brooklyn for a limited time. By August of the following year, its brief run was ending and plans to move it to Union Square in New York City were underway.

Just before Christmas in 1887 the rotunda in Union Square, at 4th Avenue and 19th Street, opened its doors to the public.

The souvenir program resembled the one used in Brooklyn right down to the pen and ink drawing on the front cover. As in other venues, it was reprinted periodically which caused only the advertisements and the color of the cover to change, with one notable exception. During the painting's run in Union Square, a veterans' event in the city inspired the stock company that managed it to produce a special cover bearing a beautiful colored lithograph by Forbes Company of Boston and New York. Portraits of Meade, Pickett, Lee and Hancock appeared beside Union and Confederate flags along with other symbols of memorialization. The late 1880s was a time for many reunions among the veterans, a fact that was reflected in this special cover.

Philippoteaux's *Battle of Gettysburg* remained on display in Union Square until April 1890. For at least two years, it competed with a non-Philippoteaux *Gettysburg* cyclorama painting which was shown at Madison Avenue and 59th Streets until November 1891. New York City had yet a third rotunda where other Civil War battle and religious cycloramas were exhibited.

In 1892, Philippoteaux's New York version of the *Battle of Gettysburg* Cyclorama can be found in Washington D.C. in a rotunda at the corner of 15th Street and Ohio Avenue. By this time, Gettysburg cycloramas produced in other studios were advertised in several cities around the country making it difficult to track the original Philippoteaux paintings from this point.

Around this time, a promoter by the name of Emmett W. McConnell, known as the "Panorama King," began to show a number of battle cycloramas, most of which were produced in the Milwaukee, Wisconsin studio. He was an ambitious entrepreneur with a flair for marketing, making statements that were not always entirely based in fact. McConnell displayed a *Battle of Gettysburg* Cyclorama at the Atlanta Exhibition of 1895. He then displayed this same painting at the Tennessee Centennial in 1897. Years later, a McConnell associate named Paul Atkins reported that "I had Paul Philippoteaux's Battle of Gettysburg at Atlanta....I did not own it however." McConnell stated, in reference to the same painting while it was in Tennessee, that "...it used to stand in Brooklyn, NY." Whether it was indeed the New York version of Philippoteaux's *Battle of Gettysburg* we may never know. But we do know that the New York version was eventually cut into smaller pieces. Some of the pieces were framed and distributed to veterans' posts. Two of these framed scenes are currently in the collections at the Gettysburg National Military Park. They bear the same striking colors and rich detail as the Boston version on display there. Some of these smaller pieces had a different fate. A short newspaper article printed in the Gettysburg *Star & Sentinel* on August 1, 1906, indicates that pieces of the New York version had "been found cut into strips and used as a restaurant tent at the opening of the Shoshone reservation."

Cycloramas truly were popular forms of mass entertainment in the decade of the 1880s but their popularity waned almost as quickly as it had risen. While three of the four Philippoteaux paintings seemed to disappear during the 1890s, a few of the later buckeyes continued to surface periodically. The last non-Philippoteaux *Battle of Gettysburg* Cyclorama was on display for the 1933 Century of Progress Expo in Chicago. Its last show was in 1936 at the Texas Centennial Expo. In 1937 it was packed up and placed in a warehouse in Chicago where it remained until North Carolina artist Joe King discovered it and purchased it sight unseen. Upon his death, the painting was willed to Wake Forest University and remained under its ownership until it was sold to investors in 2007. Careful comparison of photographs of the Wake Forest version against existing photographs of the original four *Battle of Gettysburg* Cycloramas proves that it was inspired by Paul Philippoteaux's master works but it is not one of them.

Cyclorama Souvenirs

EVERY ONE

SHOULD SEE

This wonderful exhibition. Hundreds of thousands of people have already done so, and there is room for hundreds of thousands more. **ALL** pronounce it the **MOST MARVELLOUS PRODUCTION** of **THIS AGE. EVERY SCHOLAR** in New England can learn more at "**GETTYSBURG**" in one hour, than from books in a whole month.

OPEN EVERY WEEK DAY FROM 9 A.M. TO 11 P.M.

541 TREMONT STREET, BOSTON.

Advertisement for the Gettysburg cyclorama in Boston.

Beautiful lithograph cover for a special souvenir program at Union Square, New York City.

SEASON TICKET
Battle of Gettysburg

No. _Dgw 550_ X _916_

NOTE.—This ticket will be forfeited if presented by any other person than the one to whom it is issued.

Atkinson & McConnell

SEASON TICKET
CYCLORAMA.
PRICE, $5.00.

I hereby agree not to sell or transfer this ticket to any other person.

John T. Wilson

Front and back of a season ticket to see the *Battle of Gettysburg* cyclorama. It was issued to John T. Wilson, a Confederate veteran of Company H, 25th Virginia Infantry, who fought at Gettysburg.

Broadside published in the Philadelphia newspaper in 1891 to announce the Boston version of the cyclorama showing there. Note it says, "…not the cyclorama shown here some years ago, but the grandest and most costly of all."

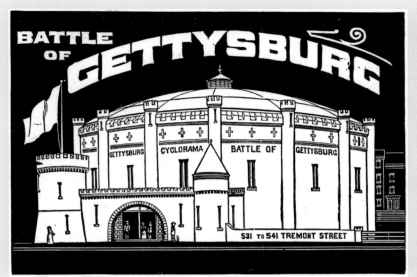

Use Horsford's Acid Phosphate for Headache, Dyspepsia, Nervousness, Impaired Vitality, and as a Delicious Drink.   For sale by all Druggists.
☞BEWARE OF IMITATIONS AND SUBSTITUTES.

Advertisement for the Gettysburg cyclorama in Boston.

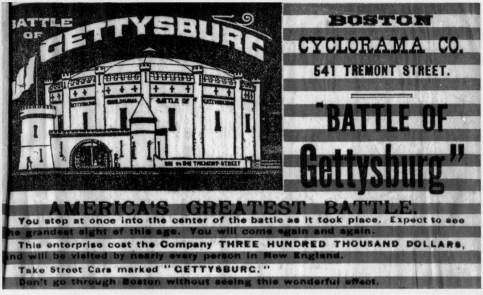

Souvenir flag from the Boston cyclorama.
These have only been seen by the author for Philippoteaux's exhibits.

Souvenir of the Chicago Gettysburg cyclorama inscribed to General Gibbon by manager Emile Glogau to commemorate Gibbon's visit.

Since the early 1900s, it was the opinion of many people that Gettysburg should be home to one of the large paintings that bore its name.

Ironically, in early 1910, a buckeye version of the *Battle of Gettysburg* was being considered for permanent location in Gettysburg. According to the *Gettysburg Compiler* of March 19, 1910, "That the world famous cyclorama of the Battle of Gettysburg is permanently to be located here in the near future by a company of Washington capitalists is confidently expected, an option on the Cobean and Tawney properties on Chambersburg and Washington Streets having been bought on Friday by representatives of the company..... The cyclorama would be one of Gettysburg's greatest attractions and, housed in a beautiful building, would serve as a great ornament to the town." This painting was produced in the Chicago studio of Gross and Reed. Plans, however, fell through as reported in the *Adams County News* dated September 17, "The celebrated Cyclorama of the Battle of Gettysburg....was sold in Chicago to Kraus and Golbus, junk dealers, for $1. This marks the end of the project to bring the world famous painting to Gettysburg for a permanent home. Within the past year a special effort was made to secure funds for its purchase and the erection of a building here."

Three years later, Gettysburg did finally get a *Battle of Gettysburg* Cyclorama.

It is not known what inspired the Newark department store magnate Albert Hahne to purchase the Boston version of the *Battle of Gettysburg* Cyclorama, thereby saving it from further destruction on the vacant lot where it had lain for many years. The acquisition, however, was probably instigated by Thomas T. Fryer, a dealer in fine art and rare books, who knew of the painting and interested Hahne in it late in 1910.

Upon learning of the painting, Albert Hahne designated A. H. Hannoch as his personal representative to travel to Boston, view the painting and report back to him. In a letter written from the Parker House in Boston by Hannoch to Hahne dated November 8, 1910, he wrote that the following day the canvas would be unrolled in order to view it. In the meantime, he had arranged for a carpenter to make wooden rolls on which to wrap the canvas for transport. He also met with individuals to look over documents and bills of sale.

In a letter dated one day later, Hannoch wrote to inform Hahne that he (Hahne) was the new owner of the *Battle of Gettysburg* Cyclorama and went on to describe the painting itself: "We have unrolled about 125 feet which has been cut into four pieces. Two pieces 27 feet wide and two only 19 feet wide, the latter being the sky......Figured each roll to weigh between 700 and 800 lbs."

The cyclorama was shipped to New Jersey and placed on display at the Hahne & Company store at 609 Broad Street in downtown Newark. An advertisement in the *Newark Evening News* on February 7, 1911, stated, "Tomorrow, after months of arduous labor and the expenditure of a great sum of money, we will reveal to the public the greatest painting of the 'Battle of Gettysburg' ever put on canvas....This picture is hung in the great Grand Court of the store from the dome to below the fourth floor. It stretches almost entirely round both courts, being 352 feet long in all...."

Hahne employed photographer Harry G. Potter to capture each part of the painting on prints. These photographs are in the Gettysburg National Military Park collections and reveal the significant deterioration suffered by the painting up to that time.

In mid-June, 1911, at the suggestion of General Daniel Sickles, the cyclorama painting was sent by Hahne to the Armory of the 12th Infantry National Guard of New York located at 62nd Street and Columbus Avenue in New York City. It was displayed there in much the same way as it was in Hahne's store. This and subsequent exhibitions were managed by Mr. Fryer, the arts dealer who originally located the canvas for Hahne. In the literature accompanying this exhibit, it was noted that "there is an effort being made to have (the painting) placed in a permanent building on or near the historic battlefield which it portrays." This is the first hint of its future in Gettysburg.

Although scheduled to stay in New York City for one month, the exhibition remained until the end of August before moving on to the Fourth Infantry Maryland National Guard Armory on Fayette Street in Baltimore. While on exhibit there in late September, the painting was viewed by LaSalle Corbell Pickett, the widow of Confederate General George Pickett, one of the leaders of the charge depicted on the canvas. This unannounced visit was the first time Mrs. Pickett had seen the *Battle of Gettysburg* painting. According to the commander of the Fourth Regiment, Colonel Frank Supplee, she recited the portion of her lecture devoted to the third day of the Battle while all around her were depicted the scenes she was describing. Afterwards, Mrs. Pickett remarked that for her it was an ever memorable afternoon.

Sometime during the spring of 1912, the cyclorama painting was hung from the galleries in the ball room of the Pension Office Building in Washington, DC. The permit, requested by Mr. Fryer on behalf of Albert Hahne, was for a period of 60 days. While on exhibit there, it was viewed by Pension Office employee C. O. Howard, son of General O. O. Howard, who suggested that the painting should be on permanent display at Gettysburg. This last showing of the canvas before it moved on to Gettysburg was plagued with problems concerning financing, management and liabilities incurred by the exhibition and the visiting public.

Meanwhile, in late June 1912 the Gettysburg Battle Picture Association was granted a charter by the legislature of Pennsylvania for the purpose of erecting a building to house the Philippoteaux *Battle of Gettysburg* Cyclorama. Hahne himself put $7,000 into the venture. A lot on the north side of East Cemetery Hill, owned by Dr. Walter O'Neal, was leased and a circular framework of steel began to appear soon after groundbreaking on September 2nd. The diameter of the tile build-ing was 120 feet and the height of its walls was 28 feet. The roof bore skylights and ventilation portals. No other cooling or heating source was installed. This may have been due in part to the premise that this building was to be temporary in nature, and that it was hoped the Federal Government would build a magnificent and permanent building worthy of the painting some time in the future.

Complications quickly arose with financing and the Gettysburg Battle Picture Association was dissolved. Its assets were purchased at sale by Albert J. Hahne and a new organization, the Picture Association of Gettysburg, was formed with Hahne as Director. He leased the painting to the corporation for an indefinite period of time.

The building opened in May with Fryer serving as the initial custodian and lecturer. A fee of $0.25 per person was charged to see the painting. An article in the *Gettysburg Times* on May 8, 1913 described the exhibition: "The world famous Philippoteaux painting of the Battle of Gettysburg arrived in Gettysburg....After many years of endeavor to provide a permanent home for the masterpiece...it seems that one at last has been found, and that at Gettysburg, where many have always thought it would be permanently located. The painting is in eleven sections and is twenty eight feet in height.....(it) was so heavy that a number of trips in a large wagon were required to convey the various sections from the freight depot to the cyclorama building."

Charles M. Young, a Gettysburg College student who would later become a well-known painter, did some touch-up work to damaged parts of the painting while it was being hung in the build-

Tile building on East Cemetery Hill that housed the painting from 1913 until 1962.

ing. No diorama was created since the building was to be a temporary home for the painting.

Newspaper coverage of the 50th anniversary of the battle and the reunion of the Blue and Gray veterans revived the story of the painting's glory in the early years of its existence. The *Boston Evening Transcript* on July 3, 1913, reported, "one of the most artistic cycloramas ever painted was Paul Philippoteaux's 'Battle of Gettysburg' which was for some years exhibited in a circular building on Tremont Street....The writer was often present when veterans who had taken part in the battle visited the exhibition in this city and testified in a most emphatic manner to the accuracy of the painting, showing by their intense interest and excitement the strong impression made on them by the vivid reminder of the crisis of combat....Many were the personal reminiscences of Gettysburg brought out by the old soldiers who came to see the painting. They were able to recognize in many cases the very localities where they were at the time of Pickett's Charge."

About a year after the painting's arrival in Gettysburg, Paul Philippoteaux visited the battlefield, at the request of Mr. Fryer. The purpose of the trip was to certify that this painting was indeed his work. The artist indicated that the red-bearded figure of a Union officer standing under the small pine tree with the sword across his knee was a representation of himself and served as his signature.

A copy photograph in the Gettysburg National Military Park archives shows Philippoteaux standing on a ladder, palette and brush in hand, in front of his likeness in the painting. It was autographed to Charles Willoughby by Philippoteaux. It is interesting to note that even the buckeye copies made in other studios show this figure under the tree, which supports the idea that former members of

Philippoteaux's artistic team continued to use his original drawings when working for others.

The cyclorama continued to be shown during the spring, summer and autumn months at the Cemetery Hill location although it was to have been a temporary arrangement. Upon the death of Thomas Fryer, battlefield guide James Culp took over as lecturer for about four years. Then Charles H. Cobean, an Adams County native, managed the *Gettysburg* Cyclorama from 1918 until he retired 25 years later. In 1939, it provisionally became the property of the U. S. Government under an agreement with the heirs of the Hahne estate, Jeremiah and Anna Hoover. Hoover had served as Hahne's attorney through the acquisition of the painting and the setting up of companies to exhibit it. Three years later, it came fully under the jurisdiction of the National Park Service. Incredibly, it would remain in its 'temporary' building for almost twenty more years before it underwent its first full conservation treatment and moved into a new gallery.

In the meantime, in 1948, New York artist Richard Panzironi completed an emergency on-site stabilization deemed necessary due to the deteriorated condition of the painting. Then Park Superintendent, J. Walter Coleman, was quoted in the July 31, 1948, *Star & Sentinel* that, "...the painting had 'bellied' so badly and supports had rotted away to such an extent that there was some fear that some morning the huge painting might be found on the floor of the cyclorama instead of hanging from the walls." Stabilization consisted of gluing linen bands to the back side of the canvas and drawing it back, then stapling it to wooden supports. The arrangement was ultimately detrimental to the painting. As the glue dried it shrank, causing the canvas to pucker and hang in folds. The

The artist Paul Philippoteaux posed in front of his self portrait in the painting. (NPS)

lower edge touched the floor which not only caused it to fray and rot, it prevented the natural hyperbolic shape from existing, thus distorting the layered landscape. Some new canvas was added to the bottom of the painting and a continuation of the scene painted on it to fit with terrain features. The hyperbolic shape was not restored.

In 1954, *Time* magazine photographer George Strock created the first ever continuous still photograph of the *Gettysburg* Cyclorama painting which was published in the July 5th issue.

A National Park Service initiative known as "Mission 66" provided for a new building which was initially intended to serve as a visitor center and cyclorama gallery. Construction began in 1959. And in anticipation of moving the painting into this new venue, a major conservation project was undertaken by National Park Service Painting Conservator Walter Nitkiewicz. By this time, deep cracks, flaking, and paint loss could easily be seen. The canvas was dry and brittle, and showed tears, splits, and folds. One large area was completely missing which caused a break in scenic continuity.

Mission 66 building that was to serve as cyclorama gallery and visitor center. It was ultimately inadequate for either purpose.

Nitkiewicz opened the pre-existing seams and made further vertical cuts in the canvas for ease of handling. Using the latest conservation techniques of the day, he dampened, flattened, sized and relined the canvas using melted wax and resin. The relining was done while the painting lay flat which eventually caused the seams to misalign after re-hanging due to its former hyperbolic shape. The painting's lower edge rested on the floor which promoted the development of vertical folds and eventual separation from the lining. As stated in Chapter 2, a cyclorama is meant to hang from a ring at the top with weights suspended from a ring at the bottom to maintain its natural hyperbolic shape. This painting was hung straight down like a shower curtain.

Fluctuating humidity due to lack of climate control in the new building led to further distortions and paint loss.

The uneven upper edge of the canvas was trimmed for remounting, resulting in additional loss to the original sky area. No effort was made to replace the missing sky and missing vertical portion. However, a considerable amount of repainting was done to other areas by Charles A. Morgenthaler, a commercial artist and illustrator from Hallsville, Missouri. During Morgenthaler's tenure on the cyclorama restoration project, he also painted murals for two commercial entities in Gettysburg, the Hall of Presidents and the Battle Theater. These works still exist today and show a style that differed somewhat from that of the original artists who worked on the Gettysburg cyclorama.

Additional efforts to slow the deterioration of the aging canvas in 1975 and again in the latter 1980s failed to resolve the myriad of problems which threatened to finally consume it. The gallery roof leaked periodically which allowed rain water to run down onto the painting. The lacquer covering the painting's surface yellowed. A layer of soot, emitted over the years from the ventilation system, added a gray cast to the yellowed appearance. It still had no elevated platform or diorama and there were just a few feet of sky visible above the horizon. By the decade of the 1990s, the painting was so aesthetically compromised that it did little to inspire its viewers. The illusion it was once capable of creating could only be read about in century-old accounts.

Salvation and Resurrection

With legislative approval of the Gettysburg National Military Park's 1999 General Management Plan, the fortunes of the *Battle of Gettysburg* Cyclorama finally began to change for the better. Through the vision, talent, and perseverance of a Park superintendent, a philanthropic contractor, a foundation president and a nationally known conservator, the cyclorama painting embarked on a five-year journey to return it to its former glory.

Superintendent John Latschar made a strong case for inclusion of the cyclorama painting in the management plan, due both to its definition as a very large cultural resource and because its location at that time prevented restoration of key battlefield terrain. When the Gettysburg National Battlefield Museum Foundation — now the Gettysburg Foundation — was formed to raise funds for the various projects included in the plan, its President, Robert Wilburn, worked diligently to promote the needs of the painting as an integral part of the larger project. Contractor Robert Kinsley took the necessary steps at his own expense to find out the proper way to build a cyclorama gallery and install a painting of such huge proportions. These steps took him around the world to visit other cycloramas because no one in America had the knowledge or the skill to accomplish the task. Chief Conservator David Olin, known for his skill in handling other historical art of national significance, assembled and directed an impeccable team which was international in culture and scope. All of these people and many others associated with them gave their considerable talent and dedication to conserve and restore the *Battle of Gettysburg* Cyclorama.

All of the problems mentioned above affected the integrity of the painting and were noted in the National Park Service's cyclorama treatment report. But even to the untrained eye, the painting obviously had aesthetic problems as well, some of which were odd to behold. For example, a rock wall visible to the left as the viewer faces north should have been straight and parallel to the road running alongside it. But due to previous damage and odd reconstruction of the canvas at some point in the past, the wall

Detail showing a portion of the stone wall as it originally appeared during the Boston exhibit (top) and then as it was seen in Gettysburg from 1913 to 1962 (bottom). Notice the crooked wall and former stretcher bearer carrying buckets. These anomolies were caused when the canvas was stitched together to repair damage caused in the early 1900s.

Once the original grid was located under the paint, conservators knew how much was missing and were able to recreate it.
(Gettysburg Foundation)

contained two additional ninety-degree angles. It certainly did not look like anything one would find in the farm fields of Adams County, now or in the past. Visible in the same area of the painting was a man carrying two blue buckets where he originally carried the ends of a stretcher bearing a wounded man; a second stretcher bearer completed the original scene. During a former reconstruction of the canvas, the front man had lost his original purpose and that purpose is now restored.

Comparisons between 1880s photographs and 1980s photographs reveal other changes including a missing tripod leg over a stone well, several missing or relocated men, and trees appearing where there weren't any. All of these differences and others have been corrected through the 2003-2008 conservation process so that the painting once again conveys the artist's intent.

The conservation process was slow and arduous. It is not the intent to discuss the steps in detail in this book but simply to give a sense of the great amount of labor involved. All that had

View of Codori farm after conservation of the cyclorama was completed.

One portion of the initial study in oil created by Philippoteaux preparatory to taking on the full-sized canvas. (Chicago History Museum)

been previously done to the painting in prior attempts to conserve it had to be undone before the latest effort could begin. The painting was cleaned several times and studied closely for irregularities like those mentioned above. To facilitate the realignment of its original sections, old seams were reopened. Old backing, glue and wax were stripped off, brittle patches were removed and new patches added. Approximately three feet of old canvas from the former sky area that later had been added to the bottom was removed entirely. Layers of paint added over the years were removed. Wrinkles and folds were smoothed out. Glue residue was painstakingly scraped from the back of the canvas a square inch at a time (the authors and other Foundation staff assisted with this task as volunteers). Hundreds of small areas where paint had been lost were filled in to smooth and level the surface in preparation for in-painting.

Missing areas, including a large vertical piece near the artist's portrait, were replaced and repainted using 1880s photographs of the painting in its original condition. Restoring the appearance of the newly replaced canvas where the missing sky had been was challenging because no one living today has ever seen this painting with the sky intact. Fate, however, intervened to lend assistance for this particular part of the process. The authors,

The second portion created by Philippoteaux. The third part was not found. (Chicago History Museum)

both of whom work for the Gettysburg Foundation, traveled to Chicago in February 2005 to visit the Chicago History Museum on a mission unrelated to the cyclorama. While looking through the collections files there, the name 'Philippoteaux' attracted their attentions. Two of Philippoteaux's preliminary full-color studies in oil for the *Battle of Gettysburg* Cyclorama were found residing at the Chicago History Museum! The two paintings are each 9 feet long and 4 feet high, making them match the 1:10 scale typical of those described in the cyclorama creation process. They represent two-thirds of the larger composition. The whereabouts of the other one-third is unknown. The study paintings are vibrant and contain all of the main elements found in the larger work. Philippoteaux's signature is clearly visible in the lower right margin of each canvas. These two studies, along with written accounts from participants, were the historical evidence needed by the conservation team to restore the long-missing sky.

By mid-July 2008, the painting was reconstructed, weighted and retouched, and the new diorama completed. With the illusion restored, all that remained was to relive the glory days of the *Battle of Gettysburg* Cyclorama.

Scene from the newly-conserved *Battle of Gettysburg* cyclorama.

The Restored Gettysburg Cyclorama

This chapter presents the restored Battle of Gettysburg Cyclorama in ten scenes. Each section of the "new" painting is presented opposite its 1882 Tipton counterpart, a current view of that portion of the battlefield as well as a numbered key denoting significant features.

1882

Key to Scene 1

45. Portions of Wheeler's 13th New York Battery.

46. Union Provost Guard.

47. General Henry Hunt, Chief of Union Artillery, and Staff.

1. Power's Hill.

2008

1882

2008

Key to Scene 2

2. General George Meade, Commander of the Union Army of the Potomac, and Staff.

3. Peter Frey Farm.

4. Taneytown Road.

5. 72nd Pennsylvania Infantry.

1882

Key to Scene 3

6. A portion of Wheeler's 13th New York Battery coming into action.

7. General Hancock (on black horse), Union 2nd Corps Commander, and Staff.

8. Little Round Top.

9. 19th Massachusetts Volunteer Infantry.

10. Big Round Top.

11. General John Gibbon, Commander of the 2nd Division, 2nd Corps.

2008

1882

2008

Key to Scene 4

12. General Alexander Webb, Commander of the 2nd Brigade, 2nd Division, 2nd Corps.

13. Death of Lt. Alonzo Cushing, Battery A, 4th U.S. Artillery.

14. Copse of Trees.

15. Mortal wounding of Confederate General Lewis Armistead, Brigade Commander, Pickett's Division. The artist shows him incorrectly mounted on his horse but corrected the error in the last two versions of his four Gettysburg cycloramas.

16. The Bird Brothers, Peter and Robert, 24th Michigan Infantry. They met Philippoteaux on the battlefield in 1881. He included them in the cyclorama painting even though their regiment was not directly involved in Pickett's Charge. They are depicted with the wounds they received on July 1.

17. Peach Orchard.

1882

Key to Scene 5

18. Emmitsburg Road.

19. Seminary Ridge.

20. Codori Farm.

21. Confederate General George Pickett and Staff on the Emmitsburg Road.

22. Confederate prisoners being taken to the rear.

23. Emmitsburg Road.

24. Pickett's Confederate Division.

25. 71st Pennsylvania Infantry.

2008

1882

Key to Scene 6

26. The Angle.

27. Seminary Ridge.

28. Confederate General Robert E. Lee, Commander of the Army of Northern Virginia, and Staff.

2008

1882

Key to Scene 7

30. Bliss Farm Site – buildings burned on July 3rd.

31. Paul Philippoteaux, Cyclorama Artist. He painted himself into the battle scene as his signature.

32. 8th Ohio Volunteer Infantry.

2008

1882

Key to Scene 8

33. Lutheran Theological Seminary.

34. Oak Hill.

35. Brian Barn.

36. Arnold's Battery A., 1st Rhode Island Light Artillery.

2008

1882

Key to Scene 9

37. Brian's Apple Orchard.

38. Zeigler's Grove.

39. Arnold's Battery Caissons.

40. Taneytown Road.

41. Cemetery Hill.

2008

1882

Key to Scene 10

42. Culp's Hill.

43. Field Hospital, creatively inserted by the artist where no building actually stood. Other details added by the European artists were the red poppies, not grown in America, and unusually shaped haystacks.

44. Taneytown Road.

2008

To view the Battle of Gettysburg Cyclorama is to risk becoming enthralled by its artistic beauty, overwhelmed by its scope, and thrilled by the action it depicts. To be involved in any way in its conservation and exhibition is to risk being changed forever by its greatness. Such are the feelings conveyed by those who have come into contact with this magnificent painting.

Then....

A Pittsburgh glass painter named Merritt travelled to Chicago looking for work during the mid-1880s. After visiting the *Battle of Gettysburg* Cyclorama there in May 1885, he wrote to his son back home about the experience:

"Dear Son Willie,

....I went last week to see a panorama or a great painting of the "Battle of Gettysburg." It was the finest and grandest thing I ever saw or ever will see. I will try to describe it to you. On the corner of Wabash Avenue and Hubbard Court is a brick building built on purpose for this picture. It is round – you go in at the bottom in a small door – the building is about as large as the "Monongahela House" you go through a long passage (all dark) and come out in the center and go up on a platform and look around you – you are right in the centre of the Battle. All around you is everything – just as if you were on the field when the fight was going on. You can see for 15 miles all-around. Thousands and thousands of soldiers – horses – cannon – every thing in a battle – about 40 feet on every side of you is made ground and beyond that is the painting. You cant tell the difference at the first.... There is a platform about as big as our house – you can walk around it for hours and you don't get tired. About where the Rail Road is on Grove Station (when you stand on our porch) is about where the painted part commences. The ground and the painting is so finely fixed together you're scarcely able to tell the difference. It is a true picture of the Battle.... You may know how I enjoyed it understanding both painting and a Battle field.... I heard the men in the Shop talking about it. I went to see it supposing that it would not amount to much but I never was so pleased with a painting in my life as this. A part of the battle is in a wheat field and it comes right up to where you stand – you can reach down and pick the straws of wheat. On another side is some hay stacks where they are taking the wounded to. The stacks are scattered around – two or three are so close where you stand you can toss your hat on them – real stacks of hay. Old broken trees-here and there a dead horse or broken cannon wheels – green grass – the men all covered with dust – dusty roads – artillery coming right towards you as hard as the horses can run – fellows hiding in the wheat field – every thing as natural as life. I can't begin to write it all – some day you will have the pleasure of seeing it all."

(Sue Boardman Collection)

President Rutherford Hayes also saw the cyclorama in Chicago. On April 16, 1885, he wrote to his wife and included this comment:

"I have visited the Gettysburg panorama twice. It is the great spectacle of the city. I agree with the boast, 'the finest picture in the world'."

(Ford, Harvey S., ed., "The Diary of John Beatty, January-June 1884: Part IV." Ohio State Archaeological and Historical Quarterly, vol. 59, p. 180.)

General Alexander Webb, a 2nd Corps division commander under General Hancock in the Battle of Gettysburg, wrote an endorsement of the New York version of the Gettysburg cyclorama after viewing it in 1887. It was written on letterhead for 'The College of the City of New York, Cor. Lexington Ave. and 23rd St. New York' where Webb served as president from 1869 to 1902.

"April 15, 1887

I take great pleasure in giving my testimony in regard to this picture of the "Defenses of the Clump of Trees" or "Pickett's Charge at Gettysburg" July 3d 1863.

It is as near perfection as possible. The artist has placed myself & Cushing & Armistead in the foreground only to show our relative positions.

The former Right of my Command will tell the correctness of the representation – it is the best extant.

Gen. A. Webb, Bvt. Maj. Genl.
Cmd'g 2nd Brig. 2nd Div. 2nd Corps
July 3rd 1863."
(Gettysburg National Military Park)

L. E. Kimberly visited Boston for several days in November 1885. She wrote letters to her family almost daily, describing what she saw and did. In the letter dated November 15, "just after dinner," she wrote:

"Yesterday we visited the Art Gallery, and went to see the Battle of Gettysburg. The half can never be told to you about that. It must be seen to have any idea of it. We were piloted by a man who was in the battle, as a boy some 18 years old. The lady who walked with him is the wife of Gen. Lipscomb of South Carolina, a commanding officer in that battle on the Rebel side. I think it is a fair sample of grange work and a grand one to bring about."
(Sue Boardman Collection)

....and Now (2008)

The *Gettysburg* Cyclorama still has the power to capture the mind and heart of those who give in to its draw, either willingly or simply because it is hard to resist. Here are remarks from those who have had a connection with it at some point in the recent past.

David L. Olin, Olin Conservation, Inc., Chief Conservator for the Cyclorama Project from 2002 to 2008:

"Once revered for its historical accuracy and touted for its emotional draw in an age of Victorian sentiment, the appeal of the Gettysburg Cyclorama had diminished by the early part of the 20th century, as had the painting itself. The fact that we have it at all is amazing; the revised and newly conserved condition is breathtaking, exceeding even our expectations as conservators. Such an effort as has recently been put forth – removing, conserving and reinstalling the painting in a new venue (a full-size cyclorama painting) – had, until now, only been contemplated throughout the world; it has now been successfully accomplished and the results are tremendous – the painting once again speaks for itself! The viewers may once again lose themselves, if only for a moment, in the illusion of the event – the battle known as the most climactic event during the American Civil War. The opportunity to lead a team of conservators in this monumental undertaking was an honor not soon to be forgotten; the experience of seeing this painting stabilized and brought to life, remains profound. The painting represents a truly unique aspect of art and American history, interestingly separate but wholly unified. In one sense it is an accurate and well executed artistic rendering of the 1863 battle; in another it is a promotional exhibit, a commercial venture, from the 1880's – an entirely different era from that of the battle but one with enhanced sensibilities for its meaning and emotional draw. What was recently a visual platitude, used solely as a didactic display of the battle, now fully immerses the viewer into the epic conflagration of the battle, capturing them in the moment, holding them in the grasp of amazement while allowing them to experience the duality of the painting's history and meaning."

Robert A. Kinsley, Chairman, Gettysburg Foundation Board of Directors, Chairman & CEO, Kinsley Construction:

"Wow! The restoration of the Cyclorama has exceeded our expectations. I never realized it could be brought back so brightly to its original splendor and now it can be fully enjoyed by the next generation and generations to follow."

Barbara Finfrock, Vice Chair, Gettysburg Foundation Board of Directors:

"I am filled with awe at the 19th century talent in creating a majestic piece of art, at the 21st century talent in conserving it, and at the historic narrative that speaks from the painting itself. I intellectually understand that it is "just a painting," but I am overwhelmed with the feeling that I could step from the platform and walk into the fields of Pickett's Charge. It is so magnificent that it causes one to speak in hushed and reverent tones because of the painting's splendid portrayal of valor, suffering, and death."

Janice Pietrone, member of the Friends of Gettysburg, volunteer with conservation team:

"Having witnessed much of the process of restoration, I was truly overwhelmed when I saw the painting as it was completed. To see the canvas restored to its original shape and vibrancy, much as the veterans would have seen it, was quite moving. The beauty and accuracy of this renewed painting are a testament to the dedication and expertise of the conservators who worked so diligently, step by step, to achieve this result. What an honor it was to know them."

❖ ❖ ❖

Randy Grimsley, member of the Friends of Gettysburg, volunteer with conservation team:

"Over a period of eighteen months, I served as a volunteer with the art conservation team that restored the Cyclorama painting. I worked on the painting when sections were still in a state of deterioration.

Seeing the completed painting, which now contains the missing fifteen feet of sky, and the additional diorama, was a very moving experience. The visual effect that was created by extending the diorama from the painting to the edge of the viewing platform is an awesome sight. When I viewed the completed cyclorama presentation, which closely approximates what the veterans saw, I now understood the emotion that caused the soldiers to weep."

❖ ❖ ❖

Elizabeth R. Trescott, Gettysburg National Military Park Museum Technician:

"Viewing the panorama of the [Battle of Gettysburg] is to be enveloped in time-a second chance, to see and feel what went on before. Now, I know how Alice must have felt when she fell through the looking glass. It's not about what you are seeing; it is about how what you are seeing makes you feel. Its 1884 again, what a thrill!"

❖ ❖ ❖

Dru Anne Neil, Director of Communications & Marketing, Gettysburg Foundation, volunteer with the conservation team:

"The Battle of Gettysburg was one of the most fateful events in history. Too often, history is seen as events that happened so long ago that they have passed into the fog of irrelevance. But history is just the opposite—events of the past are inherently linked with contemporary times; the relevance is there, we just need to realize it. *Why would we not want to know how we got to where we are today? How can that journey not matter?* Every now and then, something appears that helps connect the past to the present and makes the relevance clear. People who fought at Gettysburg actually laid their eyes on this massive Gettysburg Cyclorama, which depicts one of the most tragic and profound moments in American history—the final charge at Gettysburg, popularly known as Pickett's Charge. When those veterans saw the Cyclorama, many wept at the sight. The Cyclorama's conservation has made it possible for millions of people to experience something the veterans themselves actually experienced. The stunning opportunity to be part of this massive effort, even in a small way by volunteering to help with non-technical aspects of the actual conservation work, offered an emotional link to those soldiers that will be difficult to duplicate. The Cyclorama's conservation will help instill in millions an understanding of and respect for the events of the past that continue to shape our lives today. That the Cyclorama and its conservation do this with a nod to the thousands who fought here and a respect for their efforts and their recollections is historic in its own right."

❖ ❖ ❖

Terry Latschar, Licensed Battlefield Guide, former National Park Service Ranger, past Cyclorama program presenter:

"You ask what the Cyclorama means to me? When I view the cyclorama, I feel so privileged to gaze upon the grandest method of time travel that the veterans could leave for us. I am so moved to stand in the middle of history and lose myself in such a magnificent display of the past, as I search the scenes surrounding me for signs of my great-great grandfathers. For me, the cyclorama is Gettysburg — and it IS my heritage!"

❖ ❖ ❖

Gordon L. Jones, Ph.D., Senior Military Historian and Curator, Atlanta History Center, member of the Gettysburg Museum Advisory Committee:

"The restoration of this cyclorama is a major historical achievement. Never before in our lifetimes have we been able to see this painting the way the original artists intended for it to be seen. Never before have we been able to fully appreciate the artists' skill, creativity and mastery of illusion. Here is the IMAX Theater of its day, now restored to its former glory. The Gettysburg Foundation and everyone involved in this project truly deserve our nation's thanks.

This Philippoteaux cyclorama is a wonderful artifact, telling us as much about the artists and the postwar obsession with the Battle of Gettysburg as about the battle itself. The little historical quirks and inconsistencies you see in the painting make it all the more fascinating as a snapshot of the 1880s.

I have watched the progression of the restoration process from start to finish. I have never seen a more talented and dedicated team of professionals. The Gettysburg Foundation and everyone involved in this project truly deserve our nation's thanks."

❖ ❖ ❖

Andrus Tonismae, Administrator for the National Healthcare System in Australia, resident of Melbourne, Australia, Civil War enthusiast:

"Some thoughts on seeing the Cyclorama in restoration state:

Firstly having seen it in its original format a few years ago, I was struck by the huge difference that the addition of the restored section of sky made to the scale and perspective of the entire work. It gave the work a sense of proportion and an impact that was missing from the old format. I recall that previously its presentation was quite dark and gloomy and the cleaning and restoration have restored the vivid colours that do the work proper justice. I could also see how effective a subtle and well done diorama in the foreground would add significantly to the presentation. On a different note, it was fascinating to see the restoration in progress and to see the bowing effect and the weighting methodology at close quarters. It was fun to spot a couple of things that hadn't been spotted previously. I think it will be a great hit with the public when it opens."

❖ ❖ ❖

Ken Boardman, proprietor of the Antique Center of Gettysburg, Civil War enthusiast:

"To be able to view the Cyclorama painting as the veterans and their families saw it over a hundred years ago – refreshed, restored, and complete as Philippoteaux painted it – is an experience for which we have waited for decades. This truly incredible experience will be available for generations because of very passionate and dedicated people, caretakers of our history. To see the cyclorama now truly helps to understand our history and see it come to life. You will be in awe as I was."

❖ ❖ ❖

D. Scott Hartwig, Supervisory Historian Gettysburg National Military Park.

"I have viewed the Cyclorama painting thousands of times over the years and never failed to be moved by it. Philippoteaux and his assistants created a masterpiece that conveys the vast scale, and the tragedy and courage of the battle in a manner that no other medium does as well. Thankfully, through its recent wonderful and painstaking restoration we can now enjoy its magnificent splendor precisely as Philippoteaux intended it to be seen."

Fast Facts:

The Cyclorama painting measures 377 feet long by 42 feet high.
That's 2,280,096 square inches.
From end to end, the canvas is longer than a football field.
Its volume is equivalent to 3 Olympic-size swimming pools.
When originally created, between 4 and 5 tons of oil paints were used.
Today, the painting weighs approximately 4 tons.
There are a total of 20,000 men and horses painted on the canvas.

CHAPTER 8

Canvas Scraps

As you have read in these pages, the official history of this painting is epic and enthralling. And as with any artifact or object that has existed for well over 120 years, its story is a mix of history and fascinating quirks. The story of this painting is not merely confined to its subject of a fateful charge during a seminal battle. Its story is not confined to its whereabouts during the years when it was "the thing to see." Nor is its story constrained to all of the renovation and conservation efforts it has undergone. Instead, the story of this painting is a combination of all of these things in conjunction with other various little tidbits that add flavor and texture to the entire story. These tidbits, like the pieces of canvas that, through the years, were removed from the canvas or taken from one area to patch another, are all a part of the larger whole. They all work together to create the larger, more interesting, picture.

An accounting of this painting would not be complete without mentioning as least some of the more obvious and interesting "scraps." In contemplating its story, you have to consider that it was painted 20 years after its subject matter had occurred. You must consider the times and social mores of the 1880s. Adding interest is the fact that the painter was European. Each presentation that was given in each city added another element to the story as people discovered a connection to

the painting that they were not expecting. And finally, with each removal and rehanging, the story of the canvas grew. Some of the interesting tidbits shared in this chapter are visual and some are aspects of the grander story that were experienced during the various presentations that accompanied this painting.

Cobean

Charles H. Cobean, who served as lecturer for the *Battle of Gettysburg* Cyclorama from 1918 to 1942, gave an interview to NPS historian Alfred Mongin in 1941 when Cobean was 77 years old. He talked with fondness about some of the things he remembered. For example, he said that he was often questioned about whether he thought the Boston version of the painting was painted in that city or in Paris (as the later souvenir programs claim). Cobean remembered William Tipton telling him the artist preferred to go back to his studio in Paris because that's where his equipment was. Then Tipton went on to tell Cobean that he received letters periodically from Philippoteaux as he worked on the painting in Paris.

Cobean said that he sometimes kept the building on East Cemetery Hill open for up to 12 hours if people continued to come in. One Sunday he had lectured to a total of 999 visitors and as he was closing, he wished there had been one more. Just then, a man came in and asked to see the painting. Even though it was late, he was happy to give the lecture to the 1000th visitor that day.

He mentioned that he had seen the *Battle of Gettysburg* painting while it was displayed in its original rotunda in Boston and he liked the sturdiness of the building. He also said he thought the painting was so beautiful then and he regretted that it had not been taken care of properly. He also saw several other cyclorama paintings in Philadelphia and Boston.

With Blind Eyes

A story has often been told about a blind man's visit to the cyclorama platform. It is reprinted here from the original article found in the *Elyria Democrat* (Elyria, Ohio) on August 23, 1888:

On Saturday last an old man with silver hair was led into the Cyclorama of Gettysburg by a bright-faced little miss in a jaunty gypsy hat and dress and sat down while she described to him the features of the picture in detail, occasionally asking her a question or shaking his head slowly as if in doubt of the accuracy of her account. She had described to him in her own way the onrush of Pickett's men and the hand-to-hand conflict at the stone fence where the Pennsylvania veterans met the charge of the Southerners, when he asked, "But where's the artillery, Mag?"

"Oh, you mean the big guns. They're over here on the hill in a row."

"All in a row?" he asked. "Yes," she replied. He shook his head.

"Look around," said he. "There must be some more that are not in line."

"Yes," she said, "there are some down here that are all upset and seem to be broken. I think they are bursted." "Is that where the men are coming over the stone wall?"

"Yes, grandpa."

"Is there a grove of trees?"

"Yes, grandpa. It seems to be full of men, but the smoke is so thick you can not see them."

"Oh. I can see them," he cried.

It was then noticed by several people who were listening to him that he was blind. The little girl said, "Oh, no, grandpa; you can't see them."

"Yes, I can," he answered. "I can see them very well, and the broken cannon, too."

The child looked at him with innocent surprise as she said, "You are joking now."

"No, my dear," replied the old man. "No. That was the last time I ever saw on earth. There was a caisson exploded there just this side of that fence, and that was the last terrible picture I ever saw, for it was then I lost my eyesight, and I have never got the picture of it out of my head."

— *New York Times.*

Wallace

In recent memory, there is no one more qualified to share experiences on the platform than Jim Wallace. After a long career in the United States Navy, Jim, originally a New Orleans native retired to Gettysburg and filled his time with several interesting jobs. One of these jobs was that of an interpreter on the Cyclorama platform. Jim served in this capacity for 14 years. His tenure ended when the *Battle of Gettysburg* Cyclorama closed for conservation.

Jim had the privilege of giving the last cyclorama show in the Mission 66 building before it closed, along with the painting gallery, in the late fall of 2005. In July 2008, he visited the viewing platform in the new gallery and saw the painting as its restoration was nearing completion. Jim's reaction, as he took in the freshly restored scene around him, was a single word — "Magnificent!" Although this was a reaction heard often from those who viewed the painting during the last few weeks of the restoration process, it was particularly meaningful coming from a man who spent countless hours interpreting it for others for over a decade and who had formed a special bond with it. He also remarked that he never noticed before how the landscape appears to be three-dimensional. This 3D effect has only recently been recaptured through the restoration and conservation process.

Wallace heard many interesting comments while on the platform over the years, some of which were very insightful. For example, several

James Wallace gave the last program before the cyclorama building closed in 2005. He worked the platform for 14 years.

visitors remarked that the painting was very "Victorian" in that it showed very little blood and none of the grotesque injuries typically seen on a battlefield. It's true; the painting was indeed "Victorian" — painted during an era of gentility when such things were not graphically discussed or displayed in the presence of ladies. And it was expected that ladies would attend Gettysburg cyclorama exhibitions because it was a very real event in the lives of the generation for whom it was painted, for both men and women alike. Even Mrs. Pickett, wife of the hapless Confederate commander after whom the disastrous Pickett's Charge was named, visited the *Gettysburg* Cyclorama while it was on exhibit in Baltimore in 1911. She was moved to tears and deemed the viewing of the painting a very emotional experience. Men of the day, especially Civil War veterans, expressed similar sentiments.

Jim had the privilege of meeting a descendant of Paul Philippoteaux who came to see the painting in 2000. He recalls that they talked easily since both were from New Orleans. Philippoteaux married a woman from there, Marie Bechet, in 1885.

Jim's job in the old building was to set up the show with a few preliminary remarks, begin the audio presentation narrated by Richard Dreyfuss, and then answer visitors' questions for a few minutes before the platform cleared for the next show. Answering visitors' questions was his favorite part of the job. One memorable question was asked one day at the end of a show, just after the spotlight focused on Cemetery Hill and a few lines from the Gettysburg Address were recited. When the lights came up and Jim asked if anyone had questions, one woman surprised him by asking if it was really Abraham Lincoln's voice she had just heard on the tape.

Jim is one of a number of cyclorama historians who has heard and passed on the story that Abraham Lincoln's likeness appears in the painting. As the viewer faces the hospital scene to the east, there is a lean-to visible near the lower edge of the painting where a surgeon is hard at work. Just to the left of the lean-to and walking toward it, two soldiers are bearing a wounded man between them, one holding the man under the shoulders and the other grasping his legs. The face of the pale wounded man bears a striking resemblance to Abraham Lincoln, being carried in a fashion similar to the one in which he was borne to the Petersen House on the night of his assassination. Although no documentation has yet been found that Philippoteaux did indeed paint Lincoln into the *Gettysburg* Cyclorama, the image has been pointed out for many years.

In this detail, the wounded soldier being carried bears a striking resemblance to Abraham Lincoln.

There are other interesting features in the painting that incite similar discussion and inspire credible, though sometimes undocumented responses from interpretative historians. Below are some of them.

The Bird Brothers

When artist Paul Philippoteaux came to Gettysburg to study details of the battle and the landscape, he crossed paths with 21-year-old Peter and 18-year-old Robert Bird. The brothers were residents of Romulus, Michigan and veterans of the 24th Michigan Voluntary Infantry which served with the famous Iron Brigade at Gettysburg. They may have been in Gettysburg for a reunion or just visiting the field where many of their comrades paid the ultimate sacrifice. The three men formed an immediate friendship, prompting Philippoteaux to paint the brothers into all four of his *Battle of Gettysburg* Cyclorama paintings. The brothers are depicted bearing the wounds received in the fighting on July 1st. On the right is Peter, bearded, with a leg wound. Robert is shown on the left, his arm in a sling and his head bandaged.

Poppies

In the view to the east-southeast, small red flowers can be seen growing among the golden wheat. These are red corn poppies, sometimes called Flanders poppies, and they don't grow in North America. Most Gettysburg historians see them as products of Philippoteaux's French background since corn poppies have been known to grow on the disturbed soil of European battlefields for centuries. However, the former Chief of the National Park Service Museum Branch, Ned J. Burns, wrote in 1950 that "this is not entirely through ignorance of American flora. The flower

The Bird brothers of the 24th Michigan as they appear in the cyclorama painting.

Red poppies can be seen in the wheat as the viewer looks to the east from the platform.

provides bright red spots which the artist needed to achieve effects of distance and is a minor artistic liberty. An American artist probably would have used an American flower even if it were out of season or habitat...to get the same effect."

European Straw Stacks

The large hut-shaped stacks which can be prominently seen in the eastern view of the painting are often criticized as being entirely European in style. Besides the fact that the farmlands of Adams County were indeed settled by German and Scotch-Irish immigrants, and therefore typical of the stacking method they may have been familiar with, a Tipton photograph taken circa 1878 shows three of the same style of hay or straw stacks standing next to the Nathaniel Lightener barn just a few hundred yards from the scene of Pickett's Charge. A close look at the area around a stack in the painting reveals a number of tied bundles of

straw nearby. It is conceivable that the shape of the stack simply shows that the sides have been trimmed to make these bundles.

The Absence of Fences along the Emmitsburg Road

Much is made in modern retellings of the battle story about the obstructive nature of the post and rail fences that bordered the Emmitsburg Road during Pickett's Charge, and how they caused an undue number of Confederates to fall in that location. Yet the painting shows no such fence on either side of the road. It is probable that these barriers were long gone by the 1880s when Philippoteaux first visited Gettysburg.

Hospital Scene

In the Chicago version of the *Battle of Gettysburg* Cyclorama, the hospital scene to the east does not depict the large white building that

appears in all subsequent versions. Instead, there is an additional large straw stack in the painting and two in the diorama in front. Many visitors ask if the building in the Boston and later versions represents Meade's headquarters.

Meade's Headquarters, thought to be too important to leave out of the painting, was added based on this Tipton photograph.

According to Charles Cobean, when Willoughby discovered that Meade's headquarters couldn't be seen from The Angle, he wrote to Philippoteaux and told him it had to be there because it was important. Philippoteaux then wrote to Tipton and asked him to take a close-

The straw stacks seen on the canvas are distinctly European in appearance, but were not so different from those found in Adams County. The circa 1878 photo (above, right) of the Nathaniel Lightener farm on Baltimore Pike shows similar straw stacks next to the barn.

up photograph of the building so he could include it. While the resulting white building in the painting is fairly accurate, its location is not; it sits too far forward on Cemetery Ridge.

Armistead Mounted on Horseback

Historical accounts show that General Lewis Armistead, the only Confederate brigade commander who reached the stone wall during the charge on July 3rd, was not mounted on a horse as he crossed the deadly fields that day. Veterans pointed out that fact to Philippoteaux at some point, causing him to show the general on foot in the third and fourth versions of the *Gettysburg* Cyclorama.

The Limber Chest in the Diorama

Some of the artillery carriage and limber parts in the restored diorama came from the area under the old exhibit drum in the Mission 66 building. They had been there from the time that building opened in 1962. These pieces were taken out and cleaned for placement in the new gallery. Upon closer inspection, the relic limber chest tuned out to have been stenciled on the side of the box with the faded letters of the name "J. G. Benton." James Gilchrist Benton graduated from the United States Military Academy in the Class of 1842, and served in the U.S. Ordnance Department. At the time of the Battle of Gettysburg, he was "Principal Assistant" to the Chief of Ordnance at Washington, D.C. On September 15, 1863, he was promoted to the rank of Major and to the command of the Washington Arsenal.

General Armistead is shown falling mortally wounded from his horse in the painting. Armistead did not ride across the fields of Pickett's Charge that day. The artist corrected this image in the final two versions.

Civil War limber chest, transferred from the old building to the diorama in the new building.

The Surgeon

The hospital scene to the east shows a wooden lean-to under which a surgeon and his assistant are hard at work caring for the wounded. Oral history tells us that the surgeon is a civilian by the name of Dr. David Study who lived across the street from the site of the early cyclorama building on East Cemetery Hill.

The surgeon depicted in this detail may be Dr. David Study, a Gettysburg doctor.

Program Key

There were three different keys to Philippoteaux's four *Battle of Gettysburg* cycloramas — Chicago and Boston used the same one, and Philadelphia and New York each had their own. In an interesting marketing ploy, many of the troops' identifications in the various keys changed depending upon the geographic location of the painting's exhibition.

This is a key to one of the original *Battle of Gettysburg* Cycloramas. When cycloramas were first displayed, visitors would use keys like this one to decipher the scene they were seeing. Keys were included in the souvenir programs that most visitors purchased as part of their experience. The key depicted here accompanied Philippoteaux's Philadelphia version of the *Battle of Gettysburg*. When Boston's version was first displayed, its programs contained the key to the Chicago version because no key was ever drawn specifically for Boston. Over time, the Boston painting came to use the key for the Philadelphia version as it was a better match. It contained Meade's Headquarters and several other significant features that were changed between the Chicago and Boston versions.

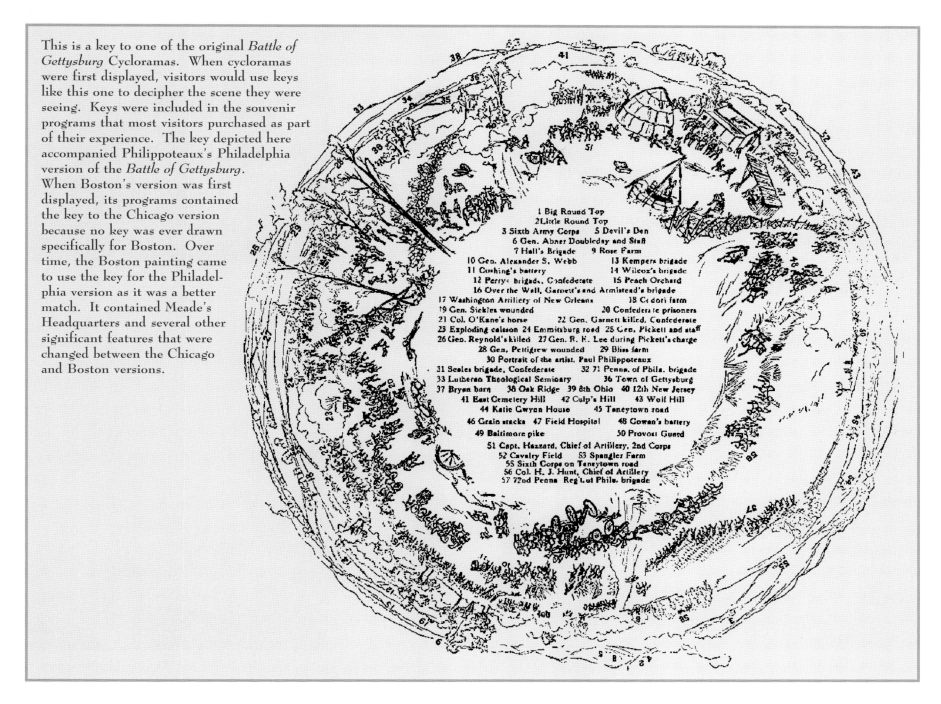

1 Big Round Top
2 Little Round Top
3 Sixth Army Corps   5 Devil's Den
6 Gen. Abner Doubleday and Staff
7 Hall's Brigade   9 Rose Farm
10 Gen. Alexander S. Webb   13 Kempers brigade
11 Cushing's battery   14 Wilcox's brigade
12 Perry's brigade, Confederate   15 Peach Orchard
16 Over the Wall, Garnett's and Armistead's brigade
17 Washington Artillery of New Orleans   18 Codori farm
19 Gen. Sickles wounded   20 Confederate prisoners
21 Col. O'Kane's horse   22 Gen. Garnett killed, Confederate
23 Exploding caisson 24 Emmitsburg road 25 Gen. Pickett and staff
26 Gen. Reynold's killed 27 Gen. R. E. Lee during Pickett's charge
28 Gen. Pettigrew wounded   29 Bliss farm
30 Portrait of the artist, Paul Philippoteaux
31 Scales brigade, Confederate   32 71 Penna. of Phila. brigade
33 Lutheran Theological Seminary   36 Town of Gettysburg
37 Bryan barn   38 Oak Ridge 39 8th Ohio 40 12th New Jersey
41 East Cemetery Hill   42 Culp's Hill   43 Wolf Hill
44 Katie Gwynn House   45 Taneytown road
46 Grain stacks 47 Field Hospital   48 Cowan's battery
49 Baltimore pike   50 Provost Guard
51 Capt. Hazzard, Chief of Artillery, 2nd Corps
52 Cavalry Field   53 Spangler Farm
55 Sixth Corps on Taneytown road
56 Col. H. J. Hunt, Chief of Artillery
57 72nd Penna. Reg't of Phila. brigade

Chicago

The photos on this page compare the four original versions of Philippoteaux's *Battle of Gettysburg* cyclorama with the version stored at Wake Forest until 2007. The Wake Forest version has often been referred to as the original Philippoteaux Chicago version but is actually a buckeye version. This is the scene looking due east from all five versions. The original Philippoteaux Chicago version was the only one that did not depict Meade's headquarters building prominently. The later three Philippoteaux versions corrected this omission. You can see how the Wake Forest version was influenced by the four Philippoteaux originals but upon close inspection, minute differences in detail can be seen.

Boston

Wake Forest

Philadelphia

New York

Bibliography

Panoramania! The Art and Entertainment of the 'All-Embracing' View by Ralph Hyde; Trefoil Publications, London; 1988.

The Painted Panorama by Bernard Comment; Harry N. Abrams, Inc. Publishers; 1999.

Canvas Documentaries by Mimi Colligan; Melbourne University Press; 2002.

The Panorama: History of a Mass Medium by Stephan Oettermann; Zone Books, New York; 1997.

The Gettysburg Cyclorama: A Portrayal of the High Tide of the Confederacy by Dean S. Thomas; Thomas Publications; 1989.

Gettysburg National Military Park Archives — Historians' Files, 1933-1965 (GETT 41151); Correspondence of Alfred Mongin, NPS Historian.

The new home for the restored *Battle of Gettysburg* cyclorama at the Gettysburg NMP Visitors' Center. Note its resemblance to the rotundas of the late nineteenth century.
(Michael Vyskocil)

About the Authors

Sue Boardman a Gettysburg Licensed Battlefield Guide since 2000, is Leadership Program Coordinator for the Gettysburg Foundation. A two time winner of the Superintendent's Award for Excellence in Guiding, Sue has a particular passion for Gettysburg National Military Park history of which the *Battle of Gettysburg* Cyclorama painting is a part. Sue is a native of Danville, PA and an Honors Graduate from Penn State/Geisinger Medical Center School of Nursing. A 23 year career as an Emergency Department nurse preceded her career at Gettysburg. An avid collector of 19th century battlefield photography, Sue and her husband Ken are the owners of the Antique Center of Gettysburg.

Kathryn Porch spent nearly five years with the Gettysburg Foundation, first as a Development Assistant and then as a Project and Program Manager. Kathryn's love for the Gettysburg battlefield led her to Gettysburg College where she graduated in 2002 with a B.A. in English. After a few years, she found her way to the Gettysburg Foundation and was instrumental in the completion of the Museum by playing a critical role in taking many aspects of the project from the design phase successfully through fabrication. Building on the lessons and skills she learned in Gettysburg, Kathryn is now beginning her new career as a Foreign Service Officer with the U.S. Department of State.

Because the identities of so many of the individuals who have worked on this painting throughout the duration of its existence have been lost to history we would like to record, for posterity, the names of all of those dedicated individuals who have worked so hard to return this treasure to the American people. In them, we have witnessed an unparalleled level of heart and dedication. Through their skill and perseverance, their pain-staking work and great attention to detail, an entirely new generation will have the privilege of experiencing this painting in all of its intended glory.

Conservation Team

David Olin
Dan Burke
Marta Burkett
Maura Duffy
Anita Flejter
Allen Forrest
Aaron Fowler
Ali Freesland
Kelly Hopler
Jim Hoston
Lisa Jarrow
Larry Keck
Wieslaw Kowalczyk
Bruce Krumbholz
Tamara Luzeckyj
Bill Mathis
Greg Mathis
James McDonough
Jessie Norris
Debra Selden

Greg Thomas
Doug Trainor
Jennifer Weaver
Ryszard Wojtowicz
Danuta Drabik-Wojtowicz
Wiktoria Wojtowicz-Janowska
Mary Wootten

Volunteers

John Zaremba
Denise Warthen
Cheryl Winkleman
John Winkleman
Diane Rhodes
Katie Porch
Janice Pietrone
Dru Neil
Heidi Myers
Nancy Hogan
Elliot Gruber
Randy Grimsley

Chris Gallo
Carmella Champ
Richard Champ
Sue Boardman

Diorama Element Donors

Jeff Stafford (canon)
Gere Bidon
Ken Boardman
William Cashin
Earl J. Coates
Max Crook
Bill Dowling
David Ebert
Randy Grimsley
Travis Haymaker
John Heiser
Stephen Johsz
Bryan Kimmel
Kelly Kline
Pat Kline

Terri Leamer
Heidi Myers
Kevin Myers
Dave Pridgeon
Sean Pridgeon
George Rabbai
Tom Ragno
Ken Raia
James Ross
Rich Simmons
Duane R. Siskey
Jay Spurr
Jerry Stiles
Karin Timour
William Welch
Regimental Quartermaster

Diorama Fabrication

Taylor Studios, Inc.

THOMAS PUBLICATIONS publishes books about the American Colonial era, the Revolutionary War, the Civil War, and other important topics. For a complete list of titles, please visit our website:

http://www.thomaspublications.com

Or write to:

THOMAS PUBLICATIONS
P.O. Box 3031
Gettysburg, PA 17325